Kriya Yoga
Continuing the Lineage of Enlightenment

Ryan Kurczak

DEDICATION

To all sincere spiritual seekers. May the truth of what has always been, finally dawn as Self-revelation. May all seeking end.

CONTENTS

ACKNOWLEDGMENTS

This book would not have been possible without the continuous efforts of Kriya Yoga teachers and practitioners, past and present, who carry on the work through their words but more importantly through their silent example. May the lineage continue unbroken.

Chapter 1

MY EXPERIENCE OF KRIYA YOGA

Just before dawn on August 14th, 2000 I met my spiritual teacher, Roy Eugene Davis, a direct disciple of Paramahansa Yogananda. It was the Monday morning meditation session at the beginning of a weeklong retreat at the Center for Spiritual Awareness in Lakemont, GA. The meditation hall was dark, barely lit by a streetlight shining through the Eastern facing glass doors. I sat quietly in the third row back with the other retreat participants waiting for the first session of the week to begin.

I had arrived early in the hall to meditate before the first scheduled meditation session. At six o'clock I heard a door open in the back of the room. A tall man walked up through the center aisle towards the altar that sat on a slightly raised platform in the front of the hall. His features were not discernable as the sun had not yet risen.

To my surprise a rush of emotion surged through me. He made his way to the front of the room, lit a match to ignite the wick of the stained glass lotus oil lamp on the altar, and my eyes filled with tears. An indescribable joy filled my heart and then radiated out to the rest of my being as he lit a stick of incense and waved its flaming end before the pictures of Mahavatar Babaji, Lahiri Mahasaya, Jesus, Swami Sri Yukteswar, and Paramahansa Yogananda that were mounted on the wall above the altar. Seeing the outline of Mr. Davis backlit by the single flame of the oil lamp flooded my being with the feeling of reuniting with a long lost friend. He then raised his hands in prayer towards the pictures and took a seat in a large orange chair to the left of the altar.

Mr. Davis began the morning meditation with the chant "Om Namah Shivaya." As he was explaining the meaning of the words to be, "I reverently acknowledge supreme infinite consciousness," I was only halfway listening. My emotions were still churning and I knew then that I was exactly where I needed to be. I knew the path of Kriya Yoga as taught by Roy Eugene Davis was my own path. I felt like I had come home.

--

Months before I had taken up a meditation practice. When I first began I could hardly sit still for more than five minutes. From the time I was thirteen, my interests were often directed towards studying metaphysical literature and spiritual philosophy, but I had never really put any of the concepts into practice. After learning of my growing interest in yoga and meditation, a friend of mine mentioned that I should read the book, *Autobiography of a Yogi,* by Paramahansa Yogananda.

I immediately purchased the book from a local bookstore and read it avidly in a matter of days. Once finished, I asked my friend if she could initiate me into the practices of Kriya Yoga as described in *Autobiography of a Yogi.* She was a Hatha Yoga teacher and I knew she had been to CSA before, so I assumed she could. Sadly, she informed me that she was not an authorized teacher. Without a second thought, I called CSA to arrange a visit during one of their weeklong retreats.

In the months leading up to the retreat, I began consciously changing my life. I meditated twice a day, once in the morning and at night for as long as I could. Many of my self-defeating habits, common to college students, I gladly gave up, much to the dismay of my friends. I began eating a primarily vegetarian diet and took new interest in health sustaining activities. At the recommendation of another Kriya Yoga meditator I knew, I began studying Ayurveda (the natural medical system of India) and Jyotish (the Indian science of astrology). Within a short period of time I had transformed my life into a committed all-encompassing practice of yogic philosophy.

--

One month before visiting CSA, I scheduled a three-day wilderness retreat, with my twenty-first birthday falling on the second day. I took a few granola bars and tomato juice, plenty of water, no entertainment and a tent. My goal was to discover where I was going in life and then fully dedicate myself to it. It seemed appropriate since I would be graduating from college in December and felt that I needed some form of purification and preparation before being initiated into my spiritual tradition.

On Wednesday, July 5th, 2000 I was dropped off on a West Virginia country road that lead to a path which took me about two miles into the woods by a stream. Here I set up camp. The weather was pleasant. The sun shone most of the time, although it did rain on the second night. I meditated as much as possible, and spent the rest of the time journaling and watching nature or listening to the rush of the stream.

By the second day, I had come to terms with the boredom that was driving me crazy and began to settle into the peace of existing alone in nature. On the third day my meditations were easy and journaling produced quite a few insights. As I sat around the fire on the third night carving a stick, it became clear that I needed to find a way to get to the "bottom of reality". I had no idea what that meant exactly, but I did know that through meditation and Yoga it could be realized. My college study of psychology and philosophy did not give any satisfying insight into questions about life, knowing inner fulfillment, or how to live with purpose. Something inside me was telling me that the practice of yoga meditation would make this clear. I knew that it was also important for me to share the path to this realization with others, once I was steady in the realization myself.

The following Saturday morning I happily disbanded my camp and made my way back up the trail to be picked up and returned to civilization. The wilderness retreat was successful. I had learned what I wanted about my future and felt ready to enter the tradition of Kriya Yoga. The following month, on August 17th, at around 7:30 PM, I was initiated.

--

During the first few months of Kriya Yoga practice, following my initiation, I found the mental attunement with the lineage of teachers to be extremely beneficial to my spiritual progress. Before the initiation, I was certain that I did not need a teacher. I felt that everything I needed to know could be realized from my own inner being. However true this idea may be, looking back I can see now that I was just suffering from egotism and lack of understanding about the positive influence a spiritually developed teacher can have in regards to accelerating inner realizations. The spiritual benefits became clear within the first year of practice.

At times when I found it hard to meditate, I learned that by simply sitting quietly and imagining an internal connection with Mr. Davis and the lineage of teachers, my mind would calm and meditation would flow easily. The influence of my connection with Mr. Davis also became apparent when I posted questions to him via email. Often I would have a question about a particular way to direct my life positively or I would need clarification on a philosophical point. I noticed that when I sent Mr. Davis an email about the query and then sat to meditate, I would almost instantly know when he replied. If it was during my meditation practice, my meditation would suddenly deepen. When I read the return email, reading the words he had written were unnecessary. It seemed that the point had already been clarified in my consciousness.

During visits to CSA, I would often request to speak with Mr. Davis privately. Rarely did I have a specific set of questions. My purpose was merely to be in his presence. In India they call this darshan. Being in the presence of enlightened company has an uplifting effect on the consciousness.

In an effort to encourage retreat participants to sit closer to the front during his lectures, Mr. Davis would often make a joke that the blessings only go three rows back. The combination of the private talks, sitting in the first row during the lectures, and participating in the Thursday night initiation ceremonies during the retreats, I always left CSA happy, peaceful, and clearer in regards to my life purpose.

The role of the spiritual teacher is to provide a direct link to enlightened awareness. It is true that we all have direct access to this enlightened state, since it is the very essence of our being. However, experience has shown that not everyone can directly appreciate this or experience it immediately. Through communication and attunement with a person who embodies enlightenment, it becomes easier. Students are able to merge their consciousness into the consciousness of the teacher, thereby experiencing—to the degree they are receptive—the state of consciousness the teacher experiences.

It is also important to remember that the spiritual teacher is not an idol to be worshipped. In my experience attending various retreats and speaking with participants, it is common for the teacher's personality to be deified. The spiritual teacher is an example to be emulated. The teacher exists to show the way to one's own inner realization of the truth. Every person has an ego and personality with which to function in the world. The personality is not the important part of the teacher. It is the inner state of realization they embody and which they can share with receptive students that is most important. Respect for the spiritual teacher is necessary. Blind faith and worship are not.

The years following my first initiation into Kriya Yoga were blessed with blossoming inner realizations, and a sense of peace that deepened with each meditation practice. My practice included two meditations a day, one in the morning and one at night. When possible I would schedule a third at mid-day. Most of my reading turned towards the study of *Life Surrendered in God (A Commentary on the Yoga Sutras)*, *The Eternal Way*, and *The Science of God-Realization* by Roy Eugene Davis and various books and courses on Vedic sciences by David Frawley.

I found that the information put forth to guide a seeker of truth on the spiritual path has validity when it comes from an authentic source. The only requirement of the seeker is to actively attempt to learn, apply what is learned, and be receptive to truth to the best of their ability. The rest will unfold naturally from within the students own consciousness. At first, much of the information in these texts was hard for me to assimilate. But through dedicated meditation practice, and applying what I read to the best of my ability, the ideas became clear and simple. For example, the dynamics of how the individual mind relates to cosmic mind began as a purely intellectual understanding, but later blossomed into an experiential knowing that has had a very practical impact on my life.

--

During those first five years of practice, every few months, I would take the 9-hour drive from my home in West Virginia down to Lakemont, Georgia, to attend retreats at the Center for Spiritual Awareness, and to visit with Mr. Davis privately. Through my own consistent daily practice at home, and the regular visits to be with Mr. Davis, my life experience grew lighter, and my understanding of metaphysical and spiritual principles became clearer.

On July 30th, 2005 I was ordained by Mr. Davis as a Center for Spiritual Awareness minister. Kneeling before him, with both his hands on my head, he gave me his blessing to teach the practices of Kriya Yoga.

For seven years, I traveled to various Unity Churches and Yoga Studios within driving distance of my hometown, giving talks on meditation and spiritual practice. On occasion I would conduct Kriya Yoga initiation services for small groups of sincere participants.

Finally, after moving to Asheville, North Carolina, Mr. Davis suggested the possibility of starting a meditation center there, in the Kriya Yoga tradition. After three years of leading meditation groups at various locations in the area, in the Spring of 2010, Center for Spiritual Awareness of Asheville was established in West Asheville. For a year and a three months, I served as Senior Minister leading the majority of the services, with the support and assistance of Michael Getch, who had been ordained by Mr. Davis this same year. Mr. Getch is now the presiding minister of the Asheville center.

In August of 2011, after realizing that I did not currently have the interest or capacity to continue serving as the senior minister of a center, Mr. Davis and I both decided it would be best for me to take a sabbatical. The sabbatical eventually lead to the understanding that my life would be of better service developing my professional skills.

I currently work as a Vedic Astrologer to provide for my financial needs, and I continue my personal spiritual practice. When I asked Mr. Davis, if I could continue to teach Kriya Yoga, he responded simply, "Of course." This I do through occasional group presentations and through individual correspondence with sincere seekers.

As the years have passed, my commitment to the Kriya Yoga tradition continues to grow stronger. It is out of my deep appreciation for the tradition and its power to transform one's life, that I write this book as an offering to those who are interested in consciously participating in their spiritual evolution.

The lineage of enlightenment will only be maintained through those souls who diligently keep their awareness clear and established in realization of their innate wholeness. The practices of Kriya Yoga applied on a regular basis serve this purpose. These practices include specific meditation techniques, living a healthy life, maintaining mental and emotional balance, and enthusiastically exploring higher realities.

The concepts and themes presented in this book have proven useful to myself and hundreds of thousands of spiritual seekers before me.

Through contemplative inquiry into the material presented here, dedicated practice of meditation and living effectively in harmony with the laws of the universe, it is my sincerest wish that the light of consciousness dawn ever brighter in the awareness of the reader.

The path is clear for those who understand the importance of walking it.

Chapter 2

BASIC PHILOSOPHY

The essence of every person is pure consciousness. The body and mind are exterior vehicles that allow this essence to express in the phenomenal realms. Ordinary human awareness lacks the realization of this timeless truth.

Through blind identification with the body and mind, confusion results. Then forgetfulness arises and suffering follows. When we are not attuned to our true nature as pure consciousness life can be painful.

Many people think that life is easy in youth and as the years pass it becomes progressively worse. This misconception results from two distinct errors in understanding. Life is not a series of events or a time span of human existence. Life is the very essence of our being. Life does not get progressively worse. It appears this way because most people were never given the proper tools to effectively deal with and digest the events presented during the life situation.

This state of affairs can be corrected with effort. There are, in fact, various tools available for the task. By far, the two most effective tools are adopting a lifestyle that promotes physical and psychological well being and the practice of meditation. When these two tools are united in purpose, we can then effectively understand our essence as pure consciousness and function in harmony with the trends of the natural world.

Kriya Yoga is the path of effective living and intentional meditation practice. Based mainly on the *Yoga Sutras of Patanjali*, Kriya Yoga utilizes lifestyle guidelines common to all authentic spiritual traditions intent on realizing enlightenment. It includes specific meditation techniques that quickly and effectively cleanse awareness of debilitating thoughts, memories and energetic patterns that prevent the realization of our essence as pure consciousness.

The term "Kriya" is generally translated as a cleansing action. "Yoga" in this context refers to unification with our essence. Any action that carries us closer to the realization of our essence as pure consciousness is considered to be Kriya Yoga. Kriya Yoga embraces all enlightening traditions. In this regard, the devotional methods of any religious practice that functions to support the unification of our present state with our spiritual origins can easily be practiced along with the methods of Kriya Yoga outlined in this text.

Kriya Yoga is a method that effectively quickens our spiritual realizations regardless of our religious preference. Also note that these methods do not need to be labeled "spiritual". An atheist can realize the true essence of being. Reality remains ever what it is. Labels such as spiritual do not change it.

The scope of Kriya Yoga is broad. As mentioned earlier, the term "Yoga" by itself generally refers to any practice that serves to unite the ordinarily fragmented awareness. There are many paths of Yoga. Each path provides a route of reunification suitable to a particular temperament. For the intellectually discriminating yogi there is the way of knowledge, or Jnana Yoga. The person of a devotional temperament may choose Bhakti Yoga. Service oriented individuals can offer up their work for the world as a method of Karma Yoga. The physically inclined who are able to purify and strengthen their bodies through psycho-physiological efforts can practice Hatha Yoga. The culmination and synthesis of all these paths to oneness constitute the body of Kriya Yoga.

Jnana Yoga methodically clarifies awareness through discernment. Through inquiry into the true nature of existence, all that is not truth is cast aside. As the practice deepens, the shining light of wholeness reveals itself through the intellect of the yogi. Inquiry is mainly practiced through meditation and delving into questions such as "What am I?" The difference between Jnana Yoga and philosophical speculation is that the questioning process is given total concentration until the truth is revealed from within.

Of all the branches of Yoga this may be the least theistic. An idea of the divine is not necessary to practice Jnana Yoga; although it is possible that inner realizations may lead to this concept. Ultimately, through Jnana Yoga all concepts are dissolved. Then there is only the reality of being.

Bhakti Yoga invites the presence of divine love to grace-fully mend our fragmented awareness. By devotional worship, song, meditation, and service, the Bhakti yogi directs all attention towards the form of the divine most beloved to the heart. The energy of their love and atten-tion clears the way for clearer states of consciousness to emerge. Just as the Jnana yogis masters their attention and direct it to the goal of realization through inquiry, the Bhakti yogi does so through intense devotion. Separately, both routes lead to the same state of consciousness. To-gether the combination is unbeatable.

Karma Yoga provides a route of practice for people in-clined toward assisting the world to reach a more harmo-nious state of affairs. Mahatma Gandhi, Martin Luther King Jr., and Mother Theresa are excellent examples of Karma Yogis. Through their work and service performed as spiritual practice, the world was uplifted. In a sense, all branches of yoga fall under the category of Karma Yoga. As each individual undertakes the task of uplifting and clarifying his or her awareness in whatever way best suites them, the awareness of the whole is uplifted and clarified as well. Any effort to improve the individual im-proves the whole and vice versa. As you will learn through the practice of Yoga, there is no real boundary between yourself, the world and anyone else.

The most widely known form of Yoga in the West is Hatha Yoga. More precisely this can be called "asana" yoga. An asana is a bodily posture held to strengthen the body and improve the quality of the life force. When the body is strong and the life force flows without disturbance the foundation for profound meditation is set. Hatha Yoga primarily is a preparatory practice for higher realization. Although, practiced with alert attention hatha yoga can also produce a powerful form of moving meditation.

To practice Kriya Yoga means to engage all our capacities by enlisting all four branches of Yoga in a surrendered effort to realize the purpose of incarnated life. As Paramahansa Yogananda has said, "You are in this world for but a little while. The ultimate purpose for being here is much different than what most people imagine it to be."

The purpose of this school that many people call "life" is not intended to gather riches, rule the world, have lots of friends or gratify all the senses. If this were the case then people who satisfied these goals would be fulfilled. Through the efforts of Kriya Yoga the purpose of life is fulfilled. When the mind, the heart's desire, the work we offer as service, and the maintenance of the physical bodily temple are all consecrated to realizing the truth of our being in relationship to the wholeness of life, all is accomplished.

Chapter 3

MEDITATION

Meditation clears the mind of conditionings and elevates awareness above the influence of samskaras (mental impressions created by our past thoughts and actions, which have the potential to influence our present and future experiences). Samskaras are like impurities in glass. The more impurities in our consciousness, the harder it is to understand the world and our relationship to it correctly. When we are confused we make errors in judgment and perception, which can cause trouble for ourselves and others. The clearer we understand our life and situation, the easier it is to make choices that lead to peace and clarity.

Kriya Yoga practice is concerned with both understanding higher realities *and* with living effectively in our current incarnation. When meditation is practiced intelligently, we gain understanding of higher realities *and* we can relate better to the situations around us. We know our spiritual growth is authentic when we are internally peaceful while also experiencing greater harmony and effectiveness in our day to day experiences.

When practiced with attention, the meditation techniques described in this chapter are helpful in eliciting superconsciousness. The specific techniques, outlined in this chapter, can be used by anyone and are considered to be valuable preliminary practices for those aspiring to learn the Kriya Pranayamas, given during initiation.

Beginning meditators are advised to sit for twenty minutes once or twice a day. Proficient meditators can sit for forty-five minutes or longer, as long as the practice is alert and attentive. Passive daydreaming, slipping into subconscious states, or sleeping are not useful.

Set aside the same time each day for meditation practice so that it becomes part of your regular routine. Dedicating a place in the house or a special chair for meditation practice is also useful. It may help to have a ritual, such as lighting a candle or saying a prayer.

Consistently practice the techniques until you are superconscious. We know we are superconscious when we are no longer unduly disturbed by thoughts or distractions. We can sit quietly and calmly, yet alert and awake, when in a superconscious state.

Basic Mantra Meditation

Sitting up straight and comfortable, bring your awareness to your breathing. Take a deep breath and exhale, letting your body relax while keeping your head and neck erect.

17

Then let the breath flow in and out naturally. Do not force the breathing. Simply observe it.

Once settled and focused on the breath, introduce the mantra "so hum." Mentally chant the mantra. Hear the sound "so" resonating within your field of awareness on the inhale. Mentally listen to the sound "hum" resonating within your field of awareness on the exhale. To fully engage your attention in this process, imagine each syllable vibrating within your being.

Let your awareness be drawn further inward on each inhalation and exhalation. In time, thoughts and emotions will settle and you will experience inner peace. When this occurs, ignore the mantra. Sit in the peace generated by the practice. If thoughts, memories, or emotions emerge, repeat the technique to reestablish your inner poise.

Inner Light and Sound Contemplation

In Vedic teachings Om is the primordial vibration that emanates from the source of creation. Meditate on Om to restore your awareness to its original pure realization of wholeness. Om can be chanted audibly or mentally. It can also be contemplated by gazing into the spiritual eye and listening to subtle sound frequencies around the head. To gaze into the spiritual eye simply means to sit with your eyes closed, and to direct the gaze slightly upward as if looking towards a distant mountain top.

In a quiet place with little external light, assume a meditation posture. Take a few deep breaths, relaxing your body on each exhale.

Once settled, bring your attention up to the higher brain centers. Be aware of the space between your eyebrows and the crown of the head.

With your eyes closed, gaze into the darkness of your closed eyelids. Imagine the darkness has depth and space. Lift your gaze slightly upward as if looking at the top of a distant mountain. Continue to gaze off through the dark inner space of your closed eyes.

Now, listen for an inner sound current within your ear. It may sound like a high pitched hum, a ringing, or another constant tone. Examine this sound. Listen for any change in the sound. Listen behind the sound. Do you hear another sound behind it? Does the one you are listening to get louder? Continue to follow the sounds as they change and draw you deeper into meditation. Note that the inner sound current can be heard most easily after having meditated to the superconscious stage after using another technique or when meditating in a church, meditation hall, or similar silent place.

Initially, the sounds you hear will be the electrical activity of the nervous system, but with practice you will begin to hear the Om vibration. Allow your small sense of self to dissolve into the sounds you perceive.

As you practice this technique, while keeping your attention in the higher brain centers and looking inward, you may also begin to see lights or geometrical patterns in your spiritual eye. When this occurs, let them attract your attention. Contemplating inner light may enable you to more easily hear the Om vibration. As you go deeper into the sound current, look through the inner light. Feel that you are piercing the light, as if you are moving through your forehead into the source of the light.

Just as the initial sounds you hear around your head are the electrical activity of the nervous system, initial light perceptions are the result of brain activity. To practice inner light and sound contemplation you may want to practice the basic mantra technique first. The calmer and more internalized you are, the easier it will be.

Chanting Through the Chakras

Sit upright in a meditation posture. Bring your attention to the base of your spine, your first chakra. Maintain your attention there for 5 to 10 breaths. Bring your attention up to the second chakra. Rest there for a few moments.

Continue bringing your attention up through the chakras to the crown chakra. As you go up through the chakras, mentally chant the appropriate mantra at each chakra.

Chakra	Location	Seed Syllable
Root	Base of the spine	Lum
Sacrum	Small of the back	Vum
Navel	Behind the navel	Rum
Heart	Between the shoulder blades	Yum
Throat	Back of the neck	Hum
Third Eye	Between the eyebrows	Om
Crown	Higher brain	Bum

Then go down to the base of your spine chanting the mantra at each chakra. Repeat the procedure two or three times. Conclude your practice at the crown chakra. Then hold your attention at the crown, sitting in the silence generated through the practice.

Sushumna Breathing

To practice sushumna breathing, meditate as you normally do. When the mind is calm and the emotions settled, put your attention in your spine. Feel your spine, from the base to the crown chakra. Imagine a hollow tube within the spine.

Breathe slightly deeper than normal, and in a relaxed manner. As you inhale, use a gentle act of will to pull your life force up through the hollow tube in your spine. If you do not feel a sensation of prana ascending through the spine, imagine what it would feel like. When the inhalation is complete the pranic current will be in the crown chakra. Hold your breath for a second, and then exhale easily and without force while noting the descending flow of the current. Let the breath exhale of its own accord. Do not force the breath out. Let the energetic current flow back down your spine like water.

When silence prevails in your awareness and you are absorbed in existence-being, pull the current up to the top of the head one last time. Let your breathing occur naturally. Keep the current and your attention in the crown chakra. Sit in the silence until you conclude your meditation practice.

Recommended Meditation Routine

To get the most benefit from meditation, practice can be scheduled once or twice a day. Twenty to thirty minute meditations are good to allow the body to relax and to refresh the mind and nervous system. Longer meditations can enable the meditator to experience more refined states of consciousness and enable more effective contemplation. Meditating twice as long as usual once a week or once every two weeks, allows experience of the deeper aspects of practice.

20 Minute Meditation Routine

Decide beforehand on two techniques that will be used during the practice session. Set a timer for twenty minutes. Sitting up straight, begin with a silent affirmation or prayer acknowledging the divine in whatever way you conceive it. Then begin your first meditation technique.

Practice for several minutes to allow the mind and emotions to settle. Once the emotions and mind have settled, disregard the technique, simply sitting quietly, enjoying the tranquil after effects.

After abiding in the inner stillness, begin technique number two. As before, practice until you are once again settled in inner stillness. Then let go of the technique and sit quietly until the duration of the practice session is over. Conclude and go about your day.

45-60 Minute Meditation Routine

Decide on three techniques that will be used during the practice session. Set a timer for the appropriate amount of time. Sitting up straight, begin with a silent affirmation or prayer acknowledging your concept of the divine. Then begin your first meditation technique. Practice for 8-10 minutes to allow the mind and emotions to settle. Once the emotions and mind have settled, disregard the technique, simply sitting quietly, enjoying the tranquil after effects.

After abiding in the inner stillness, begin technique number two. As before, practice until you are once again settled in inner stillness. Then let go of the technique and sit quietly. As you sit in the silence, it can be helpful to keep your attention in the forehead (the frontal lobes of the brain, or the spiritual eye center) or at the crown of the head. This will help you remain alert yet relaxed, lift you above subconscious conditioning and mental chatter, and encourage superconsciousness.

When you are inclined, begin your third meditation technique. As before, give your attention to the technique for 8-10 minutes and then let it go. Resting with your awareness in the higher brain centers.

After your practice has concluded, spend a few more minutes sitting, radiating compassionate good will to the people in your life, to the inhabitants of the world, and throughout the entire planet. Generate a feeling of peace and happiness, and imagine all of consciousness permeated with that sense of fulfillment. Then go about your day, fulfilling your duties.

Helpful Tips

- Do not meditate lying down, as that will encourage sleep.
- Make sure you are well rested. Passive meditation or nodding off into a semiconscious state is not conducive to Self-realization.
- It is better to meditate for shorter periods, multiple times throughout the day in an awake state, than it is to meditate for longer periods of time while fighting to stay focused and awake and only partially engaged in intentional practice.
- Be aware of how the foods you eat affect your meditation. Do certain foods encourage sleep or passivity? Sometimes individuals find that garlic, onions, meat or sugar consumption can encourage grogginess or lack of ability to focus. This is not the case for everyone, but experience will give you the information needed.
- Take notice of how your regular choices of entertainment affect your meditation. Are you distracted by memories or thoughts caused by your consistent choice of entertainment? Experiment balancing your meditation practices with recreational needs for optimal results.
- Meditate every day at the same time if possible. This will condition your body and mind to quickly move into a meditative state.
- Have a reason to meditate. If you have a clear reason that makes your practice important to you, you will be more inclined to make time for it.

W. RYAN KURCZAK

Chapter 4

AYURVEDIC LIFESTYLE

In Ayurveda, the ancient healthcare system of Indian origin, health is achieved through self-knowledge. By knowing how your body and mind work and respond to the environment you can learn what supports health and what does not. Spiritual practices and yogic techniques work much better when the body is sound and healthy. A healthy body creates less distractions to our goal of Self-realization and inner peace.

Ayurveda provides a system referred to as the Tri-Dosha theory. It gives useful information and guidelines enabling a person to effectively relate to their environment. The three Doshas are variations of the prana, or life force, that creates the body. These are Pitta, Vata, and Kapha. Everyone possesses a portion of each of these to some degree, and that proportion creates the mind/body constitution. By understanding the qualities and relative predominance of the Doshas in the body you can effectively learn how to keep them in balance. Balance of the Doshas is the key to health and developing your innate vitality.

The Doshas are forces that create the physical structure of the body and the environment. In Ayurvedic theory, each Dosha is seen to have a certain quality, function and location in the body.

The quality of Vata is similar to the wind. It is agitated, subtle, rough, cold, light, and dry. Sensations, substances and experiences that possess these qualities can aggravate Vata Dosha. Vata Dosha helps keep the senses balanced, governs exhalation and inhalation, gives the ability to move and discharge waste. It is located in the body in the thighs, hips, ears, bones, skin, and primarily the colon. When Vata is disturbed, these aspects of our health can be disturbed as well.

The quality of Kapha is similar to water and earth. It is soft, fixed, sticky, dull, heavy, cold, and wet. Kapha Dosha helps to hold together the joints, gives stability of mind and body, lubricates, and conserves and restrains the other Doshas. It resides in the chest, throat, head, pancreas, sides, lymph, fat, nose, tongue and primarily the stomach.

Pitta is similar to fire. It is oily, sharp, hot, light, sour in smell, mobile, and liquid. Pitta Dosha is the fire that cooks and processes things. It governs digestion, perception, hunger, thirst, complexion, intelligence and courage. Pitta primarily resides in the small intestines. It is also located in the stomach, skin, blood, lymph and eyes. We know when Pitta is healthy when these aspects of our body are balanced.

Begin looking at the world in reference to the Doshas. They exist everywhere. Memorize the qualities of the Doshas and then try to categorize the foods you eat and the environments you find yourself in. Think about your disease tendencies in light of the Doshas and try to determine what Doshas are being aggravated through them.

If you are familiar with anatomy and physiology begin thinking about how each organ or tissue relates to the Doshas. The idea is to understand the world around and within you in regards to the Tri-Dosha theory. By doing this, you open yourself to the subtle laws of existence and can then consciously decide to live in accord with them.

Every person has a unique Doshic constitution, and one is not better than another. Each constitution has its own strengths and weaknesses. In the current Western culture most people are overweight with the desire to be underweight. It is helpful to keep in mind that the goal is perfect balance, perfect health, and not a superficial ideal. As you learn about the Doshas you will learn which ones have a tendency to be thin, average, and stocky. If you are overweight and apply these Ayurvedic principles you may find that you do, in fact, lose weight. Also, if you are unduly thin, you may find that you gain weight. Remember, the goal is not to change to fit a societal stereotype. The goal is to optimize your health and life force capacity.

There are numerous books with charts and tables that can help you get an understanding of your mind/body constitution. These books are good, but ideally it is best to visit a skilled and established Ayurvedic practitioner to determine your Dosha. However, you can use the information below to gauge your general Ayurvedic constitution.

Descriptions of the Doshas

Vata

In Vata types the wind element is said to predominate. Vata is dry, light, cold, rough, subtle, mobile or agitated. People with a Vata constitution tend to be **very tall** or very short. They are bony with low weight and prominent veins. Their eyes are often small and dry. They have dry skin and hair and suffer from constipation, a drying out of the bowels. Perspiration seldom occurs unless nervous. Vata types are generally nervous and suffer mainly from nervous disorders. This could be in the form of tremors, insomnia or indigestion. Intestinal gas and bloating are common. Their digestive capacity fluctuates. Sometimes their digestion works well, sometimes it doesn't.

Vata types are **very mobile.** They like to be active and moving. Although athletic they seldom have much stamina for strong types of sports. Their bones are easily broken and **stiffness is common in** the joints.

Environmental factors that irritate Vata types deal mainly with **cold, damp and windy places.** Headaches are common and pain is the predominant symptom reported.

For a Vata type to be comfortable gentle, warm and pleasant environments are appropriate. Anything harsh or abrasive, like excessive media exposure, can disturb Vata.

Psychologically Vata types suffer mainly from fear. Their minds are quick and sometimes erratic. They can grasp concepts quickly but often forget things over the long term. They suffer from over exertion in thought or deed, and so need to learn to reign in their energies and rest frequently.

Vata types are very communicative and excel in the realm of teaching and media. Their mobile communicative nature makes them very sociable and may create an excellent musician. Vata types are very flexible and adaptable. They can change quickly and respond effectively when they are not overwhelmed by their own energy or the energy of others, as they are very sensitive.

Pitta

In Pitta types the fire element predominates. Pitta attributes are a little oily, sharp or penetrating, hot, light, unpleasant in odor, mobile, and liquid. Pitta is our warmth and ability to digest things. Most people predominating in Pitta will be of average build with good muscles. They have hot skin and are prone to infections, rashes, and inflammations. Their digestion is strong. Fire represents our capacity to process and cook what we take in. Pitta types generally have a strong digestive fire when healthy, giving them the ability "to digest nails." Pitta types may be sensitive to the sun and have a tendency to wear sunglasses. Due to their high heat, their hair may thin and gray early. Their skin is often fair and eyes of a lighter shade. Heart attacks and acne are also common.

Even though they have a good digestive capacity they are prone to heartburn, hyperacidity, hypertension and ulcers. All of these indicate an excessive fire in the body. Their urine, stool and sweat may have a yellowish color to it which is slightly malodorous. They can suffer from toxic blood and may bleed and bruise easily. Environmentally, excessive heat and light can cause problems. Areas of coolness and shade are preferred.

Psychologically Pitta types are competitors. They love winning and disdain losing. They are generally the movers and shakers. They are very intelligent and perceptive. When directed to higher purposes they can be warriors for the truth. They are good at preaching and persuasion, and things of a technical nature. Anger and violence are their main vice. Compassion is not their strong point.

Kapha

Kapha types are of the water element. Kapha is wet, cold, heavy, dull, sticky, soft, and fixed. Kapha makes up our flesh, secretions and water in our body. Kapha types are generally stocky and hold more weight than the other types. Kapha usually manifests with large white eyes and teeth. Their face is round and their skin is thick. They have more hair than the other types and tend to have dark hair and eyes. Their digestion is slow but steady. Their main disease tendency revolves around phlegm and congestion such as tumors, obesity, asthma and colds. Kapha types sleep easily and deeply. Losing weight is often a problem. Usually Kapha types don't move much. Once they become active they have strong endurance and can benefit from physical labor. Kapha types prefer hot, light and dry areas. When placed in a damp and cold setting they often suffer. Movement and stimulation helps keep them in balance. A sedentary stationary lifestyle is not recommended.

Kapha types are very devoted and loyal. They make great providers and parents. Kapha types have strong voices and sweet speech. They make good cooks and homemakers. Thinking out of the box is not their strong point and prefer to remain in well-established and traditional groups. They often remain close to their families and seldom relate well to outsiders. Change and novelty can be difficult for them.

Their main vice is desire and greed. Kapha types like to accumulate and acquire. Unchecked this can cause emotional disorders. Mentally it takes them a long time to learn things, but once something is learned they never forget. They are good with concrete and less abstract thought forms.

Remember that each one of us is made up of different proportions of all of these Doshas. Even though one type may predominate, you may find characteristics of other types that apply to you as well. This is not a rigid science.

Learn about all the Doshas and balance your primary Dosha through supportive lifestyle choices. If you start to feel an imbalance in a secondary Dosha, try balancing that one temporarily. Proper foods, exercise and intake of impressions help to balance the Doshas.

As the seasons change or our environment shifts we must learn to adapt to the changes. A perfectly healthy Vata type could come down with a Kapha-like cold if they do not adjust well to environmental factors that exacerbate Kapha. For now, begin looking at your body and environment as a continuum each with a distinct effect on the other.

Food Lists for Different Constitutions

In Appendixes A, B, and C you will find lists of different foods that help balance each of the Doshic constitutions. They are not meant to be prescriptive, but to merely act as a guide. Always consult with an established Ayurvedic practitioner for information specific to your particular mind body constitution.

Diet and Herbs

In addition to the breath, diet and herbs are the main vehicles for taking prana into our bodies. The right kinds of food can build strong tissues and support the proper chemical balance throughout the glands and organs. Herbs provide a subtle nutrition to the body that can support its proper functioning over the long term. They are similar to vitamins, although they are much gentler on the body. The best types of foods to eat are fresh whole foods that are organic. These do not overly tax the body by having to sort out preservatives, hormones or antibiotics from the nutritional aspect of the food. When food is fresh there is still prana in it. The prana from fresh food can then be directly utilized in the body. The uses of medicinal herbs are beyond the scope of this book, yet are worth exploring to support health and well being.

Digestion is key to good health. When the digestive fire is strong it can effectively extract the nutrients from food and burn up any toxic substances before they enter the tissues of the body. Each constitutional type can utilize a variety of specific foods and herbs to keep the digestive fire strong and balanced. With regard to herbs, there are three simple formulas that can be helpful – one for each constitution. According to Ayurveda these herbs can be powdered and mixed together in equal parts, and then taken as tea. Alternatively a teaspoon of them can be taken in powdered form after meals. The formulas follow:

Vata Formula = Cardamom, Cumin, Fennel, and Asafetida

Pitta Formula = Cumin, Fennel, and Coriander

Kapha Formula = Black Pepper, Dried Ginger Root Powder, Fenugreek, and Cumin

The use of these herbs along with a healthy whole foods diet utilizing the foods recommended for your specific constitution, are a great way to begin living an Ayurvedic lifestyle.

Note, just because a food is labeled "should be avoided," doesn't mean you have to cut it completely out of your diet. If you are living a balanced life and are relatively healthy your body can probably handle an indulgence in a forbidden food here and there. Do your best, but avoid fanaticism.

The Gunas

The Gunas are the primordial forces that arise from the most basic aspects of consciousness. Their existence cannot be perceived directly, but can only be felt through their influence. As subtle forces the Gunas govern different states of existence. Their interplay is what gives rise to our experiences and perceptions in life. They define our primary motivations and the functioning of our minds. Each Guna has its place and performs specific functions in the relative world. They are all necessary to gain the experiences in life that help us learn and grow.

According to David Frawley in his Ayurvedic Healing Course, "All objects in the world are different combinations of the three Gunas. Hence the three Gunas give us the key to all forms and processes in life."

Kriya Yoga, as described in the *Yoga Sutras of Patanjali* helps us cultivate Sattva Guna, as this provides the foundation for permanent Self-Realization.

Sattva Guna makes it easier to consciously appreciate the innate intelligence of Pure Consciousness. It is luminous and harmonious. Through Sattva Guna the soul awakens from its ignorance and realizes its true potential. Sattva

Guna gives true happiness as it directs the soul towards the bliss of Self-realization rather than the temporary pleasure/pain cycle of transient desires. Through our appropriate practices of yoga, we develop Sattva Guna.

Rajas Guna is the state of energy and activity. It provides the turbulence, distraction and changes in life. Through its constant outward motion it burns itself out. Rajas Guna is the primary motivating force behind self-seeking actions. In this way it creates pain and suffering. When Rajas Guna dominates in awareness, constant stimulation is needed to keep the mind happy. The soul's attention is directed away from being, toward change and novelty.

Tamas Guna represents the heavy binding inertia of the material world. The main action of Tamas is obstruction, death, and delusion. When Tamas predominates the soul takes itself to be the physical body. It lacks motivation for change or improvement. This force can be seen in people who would rather remain in a rut at the mercy of their circumstance, rather than find a way out or seek a cure for their problems.

Health occurs through the cultivation of Sattva. Disease arises from the predominance of Rajas and Tamas. Rajas disturbs our prana and diffuses our vitality. It can be seen in the lives of people who always need more, who can never sit still, or who suffer from constant drama. Tamas creates disease through ignorance, which leads to decay and death. Tamas predominates in individuals who have no awareness or interest in what sustains health and happiness. Sattva provides a harmonizing intelligence that allows a person to perceive clearly and function effectively without delusion.

As stated earlier, all the Gunas have their place. If a person has a Tamasic nature it is necessary to cultivate Rajas in order to stir them into action and into seeking ways of improvement. Once motivated and moving on the right path, Sattva is needed to prevent dissipation and a future fall back into Tamas from exhaustion. A higher form of Tamas can be utilized to maintain the stability of Sattva. Sattva can then be further refined by a higher form of Rajas, that keeps the mind from becoming dogmatic and rigid in life. Tamas and Rajas are said to be in their "higher form" when they are intelligently directed towards maintaining a Sattvic state.

So you see, the Gunas are a complex interplay of forces that creates and sustains our reality. The idea is to move from Tamas to Sattva. Then we are able to utilize the higher functions of all the Gunas to dance freely with the forces of life, while still maintaining a balanced existence. This will provide health of a lasting sort. It will strengthen and sustain our prana and create the state of being needed to help other people find harmony and healing within themselves.

The Mind and Emotions

The mind is the main vehicle we use in all that we do. Yet few of us know how to use it or care for it properly. The mind is the vehicle in which our awareness is placed at birth. All psychological problems are the consequence of a wrong use of the mind. Learning the right use of the mind not only resolves our psychological problems but it also directs us to our higher potential of Self-realization. We can then transcend the mind, which is inherently limited.

The mind is an object that can be observed. Most of us have never taken the time to observe it. Imagine your thoughts are a stream and you are on a bank watching them drift by. Just watch them and do not judge them or interfere with their movement. These thoughts provide the substance of mind. By taking this witnessing attitude we can easily become aware of the mind's activities. However, as long as we are caught up in the mind's activities we cannot see what the mind is. This is similar to how we cannot observe what is happening in a movie theater if we are engrossed in the movie. The mind belongs to us but it is not an indicator for who we ultimatly really are. This is intuitively known and demonstrated when we speak of "my mind." Our awareness is who we really are. Our mind is an instrument of this awareness.

The mind derives information from the external world via the senses. It is the main instrument we use to function in life. It is the instrument of knowing devised by cosmic intelligence to enable our awareness to gain life experience. Psychological problems arise primarily from our failure to recognize that the mind is only a tool. We become so caught up in the mind and its compulsive patterns of thought about who we are and what we should be doing, that we severely limit our freedom as spiritual beings. We become slaves of the mind, lose control of our destiny, and are subject to the uninformed desires of the mind and senses.

As mentioned earlier, the mind is directed by the Gunas that are predominant in our mental nature. We must engage the Gunas to heal the mind and bring our prana back into balance. In the mind, Sattva is intelligence and imparts balance. It is luminous in nature, brings about the awakening of the soul, and is the principle of clarity, wideness and peace, the force that unites all things together. Rajas is energy and causes imbalance. Rajas is the quality of change, activity and turbulence. It is a self-seeking influence that abides with passion, which ultimately causes distress and conflict. Tamas is substance and creates inertia. It is dark and dull, prone to ignorance and delusion. Depending on which of these forces predominates, various steps can be taken to bring balance to the mind.

The stages of mental healing are as follows. First, we break up Tamas and develop Rajas. To break up Tamas we wake up and take action to change. This moves us from an inert deluded nature to self-motivated action. Next, we calm Rajas so that Sattva can develop. This moves us from self-motivated action to selfless service.

Any deep-seated patterns of attachment, stagnation or depression can now be released. We recognize our suffering and learn from it, confronting pain we may have suppressed or ignored for years. The energy of Rajas helps us to break with the past, change jobs, modify or improve how we relate to others, or move to a new locale. Ultimately, we bring new energy into our lives. This is the stage of personal healing.

Rajas can now be calmed and we can proceed to Sattvic living. For this stage, openness to new opportunities and new ways of being are necessary. We surrender our pain and give up our personal seeking. All personal sorrows or hurts are released. Our problems become depersonalized. Our primary focus becomes discerning how we can best serve the evolution of humanity. We learn that life creates suffering to help us grow spiritually. Suffering is not really the proper word here, because suffering is not created by life, but by our reaction to it. Life simply creates challenges. They are like puzzles for our soul to help us mature and fully understand the truth of life and being.

The final stage is the development of pure Sattva. In this stage, we develop Love and Awareness as universal forces. We transcend our human nature for the highest spiritual nature. We no longer see our selves as human beings who occasionally have spiritual experiences; we know that we are spiritual beings only temporarily relating to the human condition. We no longer are concerned with our personal or collective problems, but rather with developing a thorough understanding of our true nature and our relationship to the divine. We now become open to all life, freely engage in spiritual practice and work to realize the wholeness of our beings on a profound level. This is the purpose of Ayurveda and all yoga practice.

Before we engage the process of healing the mind it is necessary to understand what causes mental disease in the first place. The mind is an organic substance of a more subtle nature than the physical matter we see with our eyes. It too needs to be fed, and fed properly. The mind takes in substances that builds it up. These are mental impressions resulting from our regular experiences. It also releases the toxins it produces. These are negative emotions. Food for the mind, like that for the body, allows the mind to do work. The mind, like the body, also has its proper exercise and expression, which require the right food to sustain it. Most of us consider our bodies and take care to feed them adequately, but not many people stop to consider what they are feeding their mind. People get so caught up in their emotional impulses that their minds become diverted away from the natural urge to seek light and knowledge, and drawn to seeking pleasure and self aggrandizement. To change the mind we change what we feed it.

In Ramana Maharshi's book Who Am I?, he answers the following question, "Are there no other means for making the mind quiet?"

Ramana replies, "...the practice of breath control, meditation on the forms of God, repetition of mantras, restriction on food, etc., are but aids for rendering the mind quiet.

...Of all the restrictive rules, that relating to the taking of sattvic food in moderate quantities is the best; by observing this rule, the sattvic quality of mind will increase, and that will be helpful to Self-inquiry [meditation]."

First, we apply the dietary guideline stated earlier in regards to our Doshic constitution. The essence of the digested food not only builds up the brain and nerve tissue but also the subtle matter of the mind. A balanced body provides an important foundation and support for a balanced mind. Second, we tend to the subtle impacts on the mind. These are the impressions and experiences we take in through the senses. The colors, shapes, sounds and environments around us all serve to nourish the mind. These sensory impressions affect our thoughts and feelings. As an example, consider your state of mind when surrounded by a natural setting of profound beauty. How did you feel? Now recall the last time you watched the news or an action-packed thriller on the big screen. How did you feel?

The deepest and most important factor in the nutrition of the mind is the influence of the Gunas in our life. If we surround ourselves with a Sattvic environment or eat Sattvic food we will activate the Sattvic qualities of our consciousness. The same goes for Rajas and Tamas. Rajas will activate qualities such as passion, aggression, criticalness, and agitation. Tamas will produce insensitivity, ignorance, and inertia. Sattva will provide love, clarity and peace.

Not only is what we feed the mind important but we also need to consider how the mind digests the things it takes in. Digestion is key not only with physical health, but also with mental health. If we are still hanging on to things that happened to us when we were kids or something our spouse did three years ago then we have not digested these events mentally and they become an undigested "food" mass that gets in the way of proper nutrient absorption. Bad food causes our stomachs to turn sour or makes us sick. Wrong intake and poor digestion of impressions causes mental unhappiness and disease.

Proper mental digestion depends on our intelligence to discern the truth of what we experience. If the impact of

43

things remains with us then our mental Agni (digestive fire) has not broken down and released the Tamasic or Rajasic aspects of our experience. Sattva will then have a harder time being absorbed and applied in our minds. These undigested impressions accumulate and block our perception. For example, if we see a flower in the sunshine with an open heart this image is digested easily and leaves an impression of light and peace in our deeper consciousness. If someone attacks or robs us our mind gets disturbed. This is hard to digest and leaves a residue of anger or fear. Undigested experiences will continue to be stored in our subconscious, influencing our current states of mind, until we resolve them. This is yet another reason why meditation is so important. Through meditation the mind is able to digest impressions properly, assimilate the experiences of life and rest in a Sattvic state. The more often this occurs, the stronger our life force becomes and the clearer our consciousness becomes.

In Appendix D, you will find a list of impressions and activities aimed at the proper care of the mind and senses for each Doshic type.

Once you have begun your regular daily meditation practice and have committed to living a healthy lifestyle, study and contemplation of the Yoga Sutras of Patanjali will unlock the deeper aspects of your spiritual path. The next four chapters are a commentary on this fundamental yogic text.

Chapter 5

SAMAHDHI

The Yoga Sutras of Patanjali, written sometime around the first century, contain precise information for proper practice of the soul-liberating path of Kriya Yoga. To our current knowledge, the practice of yoga existed at least three thousand years before Patanjali arranged the teaching into what we call the Yoga Sutras. His work distilled the essence of the philosophy and technique into four chapters of concise aphorisms that when contemplated, meditated on, and applied provide a direct route to personal experience of authentic spiritual growth.

Spiritual growth is a process of realization and transcendence. The purpose of the Yoga Sutras is to point the way towards the realization of the wholeness of life and the transcendence of ordinary conditioned states of consciousness. The system of Kriya Yoga Patanjali outlines is suited to people from all walks of life. It is considered a Raja Yoga, which incorporates all aspects of spiritual practice into a unified route of inner growth and realization. These aspects include but are not limited to the realm of work and service, devotional practices, contemplative pursuits, and physical practices to cleanse and strengthen the body. Ultimately all aspects of life can be profoundly affected by the practice of Patanjali's yoga system.

Chapter one of the Yoga Sutras explains Samadhi--the absorption into a unified field of consciousness. This chapter sets the stage giving an idea as to what it means to practice/experience yoga. Chapter two outlines the practices of Kriya Yoga that enable the overcoming of the obstacles to full spiritual realization. The third chapter gives insight into exceptional soul abilities that may arise from the dedicated practice of yoga. In the final chapter the states of consciousness preceding total Self-realization and indications of full spiritual liberation are described.

Traditionally, there were two methods for understanding the message of the Yoga Sutras. The first method relied on a teacher's commentary to unlock the abstract and sometimes difficult to comprehend information presented in the text. The second method relied on the student's own inner capacity to find the meaning of each sutra through contemplative inquiry. In most cases, both are necessary for maximum comprehension. The words of the teacher can point the student in the right direction to grasping the truth, but it is up to the student to gain direct perception of the truth that is implied. Otherwise, no actual learning takes place.

The format of each sutra is intended to be brief and to the point. The sutras are not intended to overly engage the mind. They are signs, which through words, point awareness in the direction of experiential truth. The mind is not given much importance in the practice of yoga for discovering the mysteries of life. The mind is a useful tool for relating to the world, and for processing and carrying information from the senses to the witnessing presence of the Self. Even though the Yoga Sutras are not intended to stimulate more mental activity, in the beginning it is useful to think about them and what their words indicate. Due to the occasionally abstract nature of the Yoga Sutras this helps challenge the intellect, develop intuition, and encourage coherent interaction between the left and right sides of the brain. After the mind has had time to process the words, contemplative inquiry into their meaning will help allow the experiential truth to unfold from within.

Diligent study and application of the concepts and practices outlined in the Yoga Sutras of Patanjali makes authentic spiritual growth easier. To gain maximum benefit from the work, first read the Yoga Sutras and commentary in their entirety. Many concepts are brought up early in the text, but not fully explained until later. Familiarity with the lay out will help comprehension. Then meditate until the mind is peaceful and begin with the first few sutras in chapter one. Think about the meaning of the theme until it is mentally understood. Then inquire what it would be like to actually experience the truth of the meaning. When the experience becomes vivid in awareness, rest for a while in the experience. Repeat this process on a daily basis after each meditation practice.

Always bear in mind that the original language in which the sutras were written is many layered, with multiple levels of meaning. What we understand now, is only one level of their application. Continuous exploration of the sutras allows the full measure of their potential meaning to blossom, leading to ever deeper understanding of the relationship of our Self and the nature of the world around us.

The following commentary reflects my current understanding of the Yoga Sutras of Patanjali. Let it be a guide in developing your own understanding of the Self-realization path.

Part 1: The Chapter on Cognitive Absorption

1. Now, instruction in yoga.

The opening sutra indicates the student's readiness for instruction. It needs to be remembered that the instruction to be received is not new or novel but is based on a long-standing tradition of practice. Patanjali was a sage in a lineage of a long line of yogis. He compiled the most potent practices of yoga into this treatise. Patanjali's Yoga Sutras are the distillation of thousands of years of research and application into the science and art of yoga.

This first chapter is entitled *The Chapter on Samadhi,* or cognitive absorption. The word *yoga* in this sutra refers to the state of samadhi. Yoga means to unite or yoke together. Samadhi is a state of consciousness in which awareness is totally united with the object of attention. In this context the unification of awareness results in an elevated state of consciousness often referred to as spiritual.

Ordinary consciousness is fragmented. When awareness is unified we know our relationship to the wholeness of life. We then know who we are at the deepest level of our being and can function spontaneously and appropriately in harmony with the totality of life.

2. Yoga is the process of ending fluctuations and changes in the field of consciousness.

Samadhi results when awareness is free of the changing waves of thought and definition, yet one is still awake and fully conscious. This is the true practice of yoga. Various techniques are employed to allow samadhi to express in one's awareness. It is important to remember that proper yoga practice is the practice of samadhi, or cognitive absorption beyond thought, and not just the mechanical repetition of techniques.

If a yoga practitioner cannot easily flow attention into a state of alert stillness, techniques are recommended to provide a means of concentrating awareness. This can be done through breathing exercises (pranayama), repetition of a word or word phrase (mantra), intense concentration on a question (inquiry), or a combination of all three. Through mastering and directing attention one can eventually still the waves of consciousness and perceive and be the eternal Self of which we are all a part and which is beyond conceptualization.

This sutra summarizes the primary teaching of yoga that when understood provides the highest liberation. Once we realize, totally, what it means to end the fluctuations and changes in our field of consciousness the rest becomes clear. All other sutras are support for this one.

3. Then the seer abides in the seer's own true nature.

The seer is the eternal Self of the meditator. The seer witnesses the changes that pass before it without becoming involved in the changes. Thoughts, actions, circumstances, people and places are all passing waves before the gaze of the eternal Self. Abidance in this aspect of one's being provides liberation of consciousness. This is the ultimate goal of Yoga.

When not meditating it is useful to adopt the viewpoint of the seer. Removing your attention from identification with the circumstances or thoughts that are immediate to the current life situation and taking the attitude of a detached witness can do this. Then watch the thoughts that pass through your mind, the emotions you feel, or the circumstances that pass before your witnessing presence as if you were watching the waves rise and fall on a pool of water. You, as the seer, are the depths of the water that are unaffected by the surface waves that come and go.

4. *Otherwise there is conformity to definitions.*

When awareness is not identified with the eternal Self, it becomes engrossed in the definitions of consciousness that seemingly limit and condition the pure state of seeing. The limitation is not real of course, because the eternal Self cannot be conditioned or limited. However, it does seem real when it is occurring.

Yoga practice weakens the false sense of identification with the transient definitions on the surface of the field of consciousness. Yoga makes stable our awareness as the depth and wholeness of consciousness, reminding us that we are not the passing waves of change. We are the field in which the changes occur.

5. *Definitions of the field of consciousness are five fold. They are obstructing, pain causing, or non-obstructing, not pain causing.*

51

6. *The definitions are evaluation, misperception, conceptualization, sleep and memory.*

The definitions that limit the pure state of seeing natural
to our eternal Self can be divided into five categories and
create two opposite experiences. Evaluation, misperception, conceptualization, sleep and memory can either ob-
struct the clarity of awareness and cause suffering or they
can be non-obstructing and not contribute to painful experiences. Fully understanding the functions of these defining characteristics of the field of consciousness is helpful on the awakening path.

When we are aware of their functions we can consciously
choose how they are implemented in our lives. This enables us to work with the constructive definitions in consciousness and neutralize and eliminate the destructive
ones. Since we are working out our Self-Realization
through a body and mind that exists in a physical realm
where limitation and definition are inevitable, until we
realize the eternal Self that is beyond limitation it is necessary to work with what is before us in a positive and
constructive fashion.

7. *Direct perception, inference, and testimony are the
   valid means of evaluation.*

Evaluation is a method by which we awaken to our soul
nature. Through evaluation we can make sense of the
lessons that are presented to us on the awakening path.
Proper evaluation insures that we learn in an effective
and efficient manner.

Knowledgeable people who are already established in wisdom provide testimony. Through listening or reading the words of people who have already realized the eternal Self we accept their testimony as truth until we have our own realization of truth.

The words or experience of another person cannot liberate us but they can provide guidance pointing us in the right direction.

Inference provides knowledge based on past experience and observation. For example, if we have found that by practicing certain yogic procedures our minds become calm and still, it is safe to say that more than likely repeating the process will bring about the same results. Or in relation to testimony, if the words of another have been proven true through our own inquiry and there is more to the testimony that we cannot yet comprehend, we could infer that in time we will be able to comprehend the information.

Of all three modes of evaluation direct perception is the only one to provide authentic liberation of consciousness. Testimony and inference culminate in direct perception. When we have our own experience of the eternal Self we then know through experience what we may have only had a conceptual understanding of before. We can read scriptures and listen to the words of others and then repeat what we have heard as if we understand what they were describing. However, until we actually experience it on our own, our realization is incomplete. Direct perception gives experience of truth and authentic understanding of its previously imagined meaning.

8. *Misperception is mistaken knowledge based on an appearance that is not true in reality.*

Misperception occurs when the mind is given an incomplete picture of a thing or circumstance. A simple example is that of a coiled rope being mistaken for a snake, or a shadow at night appearing to be an animal of some kind. In reality the rope is not a snake, nor is the shadow an animal. The mind only has partial information about what it sees and so fills in the rest with imagination.

To perceive life and its events clearly, a focused and sharp mind is necessary. This enables a person to live without mistaken understanding about the nature of the universe. In time, yoga practice purifies the mind and hones mental acuity so that we can perceive without error and learn our life lessons effectively.

9. *Conceptualization relies on the concept of language and is without an actual object.*

Language uses concepts to relate information. Language is like a sign that points to an experience. If you were trying to describe the color blue to someone who has never seen blue, the word itself would be empty in the consciousness of the person you are speaking to. Once they experience the color blue through their own senses then they would understand the concept you were sharing.

When trying to comprehend a spiritual truth conceptualization is a step on the road to direct perception. Once you have heard about the truth, let us say the truth that everything is the manifestation of an infinite consciousness and therefore everything *is* the infinite consciousness, you can begin contemplating what that means. In time, through the testimony of a knowledgeable person or through inference the concept may make perfect sense to your intellect. Up to this point it is still just a concept without an actual object, or direct experience of this truth.

When your consciousness has been thoroughly prepared to experience this truth, the direct perception will unfold naturally in your awareness. This can be related to the "aha!" moment when what you have been contemplating makes perfect sense, because you experience the truth of it from within. The truth moves from concept to reality.

The key is to not get caught up in the language of concepts, but to use concepts as a foundation to experience the underlying reality that is beyond the mind and its definitions.

>   10. *Sleep is a fluctuation in the field of consciousness when there is a thought or impulse towards non-wakefulness.*

Sleep is a physiological response of the body like digestion or any other action the body takes to maintain its integrity. Our awareness need not be subjected to the unconscious state that often accompanies sleep. Our body can sleep as is normal to the human condition and we can remain fully conscious throughout the episode.

Sleep defines our consciousness whenever the thought arises to sink into sleep and a semi conscious state. When we can remain consciously aware through our sleeping, dreaming and deep sleep states we are no longer conditioned by the body's physical need to rest.

By meditating to the state of alert thought free awareness before we retire at night we can intend to maintain that state of consciousness as our body sleeps. With practice sleep will become more restful to the body while our awareness remains stable and free of the conditioned inertia often associated with sleep. This is sometimes referred to as superconscious sleep.

11. Memory is the mental conditioning of previously experienced objects.

Memories are the building blocks of our minds. They provide the structure that the mind uses to function. Each memory is a pattern held within the mental field and within the cellular structure of the body. We relate to the world based on our memories. For most people the mind is the mediator between the world of experience and our soul awareness. What the mind presents to our awareness is what our awareness experiences.

If our past conditioning has created a painful or fearful life experience this can be changed through altering the structure of our minds. Yoga practice naturally purifies the mental field, clearing out the debris, which keeps the mind clogged with confusion. Through meditation the mind becomes still. Useless memories or thoughts that keep us bound to suffering are stripped away in that stillness.

We can consciously alter the contents of our mind through imagination. After meditation has been practiced we can introduce positive influences into the mental field to change our life experience. Through use of imagination we can create new subtle memories. By vividly imagining ideal circumstances and accepting them as real, they become new building blocks for our mind. With dedicated practice our outward life situation will begin to reflect the newly introduced positive memories and thereby enhance our life.

12. The ending of those definitions occurs by practice of yoga and non-attachment.

Through yogic lifestyle, meditation and freedom from attachment to transient phenomena the definitions that restrict consciousness are neutralized and dissolved. Yogic lifestyle puts the body and mind in harmony with the natural laws of the universe. Meditation stills mental noise that distorts the true nature of consciousness and allows the eternal Self to be experienced. Freedom from attachment allows one to identify with the changeless and eternal rather than be identified with the unpredictable flux on the surface of consciousness.

13. Practice is vigilant abidance in the seer nature and state of seeing.

When meditating we are directing our attention inward. By turning our gaze from the senses we bring our awareness to rest in the foundation of the senses and the external world. Once fully internalized we can continue going deeper beyond the constant hum of the mind and replay of memories of thoughts to the field in which those thoughts and memories occur.

Eventually we can immerse our awareness in the pure field of being. When we access this field we are aware of only awareness. We are. This is the eternal Self. It is our beingness that is not dependent on any form of modification or definition. This is the seer nature and the state of seeing.

> *14. Practice becomes firm when attended to for a long period of time, without interruption and with sincere devotion to truth.*

Just as any endeavor takes practice, so does functioning from the perspective of our eternal Self. A musical instrument is not mastered over night. Nor is mastery a point in time to be reached. It is a lifetime commitment to learning, growth and application. Yoga practice is no different.

Devotion is also necessary to proper practice. Without devotion to a higher cause our practice is lifeless and without the energy needed to sustain it. Practice of yoga devoted to realizing the truth for the good of all is a powerful combination for self-transformation and planetary service.

> *15. Non-attachment is the full knowledge of one's true nature, abiding as the seer, without clinging to objects of experience or objects described by others.*

Any thing that we can see, experience, describe or hear about is not who we are as the eternal Self, or the all-

witnessing seer. When we identify or seek to define ourselves through an object we lose our center in the seer nature.

We are always our eternal Self. At times when we cling
to external definitions we forget this. By remaining
firmly established as the witness, attachment to the transient phenomena of creation is avoided.

> *16. The higher form of non-attachment occurs when,
> due to identification with the eternal Self, one does
> not cling to the primary cosmic forces of creation.*

Tamas, Rajas, and Sattva known as the Gunas are the
primal forces of nature that sustain and energize the
world of experience. Tamas is the force of inertia and
stability. Rajas is the force of activity and dissipation.
Sattva is the force of light, clarity and peace.

On a personal level the Gunas can be experienced at the
level of the mind. Yoga primarily develops Sattva guna,
the state of light, clarity and peace, in the mind. When
Sattva guna predominates evolution is quickened. However, one can even become attached to Sattva guna.

When attached to the state of Sattva guna we are still not
completely identified with the eternal Self. In the end, we
must even go beyond attachment to light, clarity and
peace to know the eternal Self fully and without reserve.
But first, our aim is to make Sattva stable in mind and
consciousness.

17. As the defining characteristics of consciousness become less powerful, there may be subtle feelings of bliss due to partial samadhi experiences mixed with thoughts and a sense of individuality as eternal existence.

As we wake up on the spiritual path it can begin to feel like our burdens have been lessened and we are freer in life. We may experience greater sense of being present in the now which causes subtle feelings of joy. All of this may occur while we are still identified with our current personality and body. We may experience partial awakening, halfway experiencing the truth of our nature, while retaining a limited sense of individuality.

18. Higher samadhi leaves a positive form of conditioning on the mind.

Lower samadhis are partial. Truth may be experienced while being mixed with thoughts, feelings, or other experiences. A lower samadhi experience is helpful as encouragement to continue practice, but does not have the full purifying effect of higher samadhi.

When, through dedicated Yoga practice, we experience complete immersion in the eternal Self our consciousness is purified. All experiences leave a form of conditioning on the mind, which can limit or define our consciousness. The experience of a higher samadhi differs from other experiences in that it leaves a conditioning that frees and liberates the consciousness.

Through higher samadhis our consciousness experiences pure unadulterated truth and the mind/body unit is cleansed of restrictive conditioning. Through repetition of this experience we eventually begin to permanently dwell in the ever-present liberated state of consciousness.

> *19. When samadhi is partial, one may move on to higher realizations or may again fall back into relationship with nature.*

Partial unification with the totality of pure being can lead to complete realization of the eternal Self, or it can be a temporary state of consciousness before falling back into identification with the ego and individualized awareness. When samadhi is partial there is a mixture of truth and remaining delusion.

Through focused attention we can give our awareness fully to the truth and thereby move closer to complete samadhi. If our powers of discrimination are not yet refined or we lack the energy to sustain our practice we may fall back into delusion.

> *20. Higher samadhi is proceeded by faith, energy, non-obstructing memories of previous samadhi experiences, cognitive absorption and revelation of inner knowledge.*

Faith provides the proper mental framework to allow higher samadhi to unfold. Without faith there is no confidence that a higher samadhi experience can occur. Even though belief in higher samadhi is not completely necessary, it is a helpful facilitator.

Sufficient energy provides the fuel for the body and mind to process the higher samadhi. If the body is weak or the nervous system unrefined from lack of yoga practice, or if the mind has no energy to sustain concentrated attention higher samadhi is more difficult to realize.

Recall from sutra 11 that memory is a form of conditioning of consciousness. Recall from sutra 18 that higher samadhi leaves a positive conditioning on consciousness. By remembering past samadhi experiences we can anticipate a similar experience. Once established the experience is fully remembered, we can imagine what it would be like to move on to higher samadhi experiences where awareness is even clearer and more serene.

From here we can engage our cognitive facilities to be absorbed by the memory and imagination. Then with patient attention wait for the spontaneous revelation of inner knowledge and insight.

21. *When frequency of practice is intense, higher samadhi is near.*
22. *Frequency of practice may be mild, moderate or extreme, which correlates to the nearness of higher samadhi.*

As with all endeavors, the more skillful effort that is given to any endeavor, the more effective the results. A yogi who practices frequently and applies all possible energy to the practice will gain results sooner.

It must be remembered that the effort must be applied intelligently and not be distorted by misperceptions. Practice of meditation and other lifestyle enhancing routines will work most effectively when performed with a surrendered attitude. Trying to force samadhi to occur through strenuous meditation is a kind of distortion. The personal ego is in the way. Forceful meditation or fanatical lifestyle regimens are best to be avoided. Practice can remain intense while maintaining a relaxed and patient attitude. Then the way is clear for samadhi to occur.

> 23. *Samadhi is also near when there is perfect alignment with Ishvara.*

In Sanskrit this sutra refers to, "Ishvara pranidhanad". Ishvara is the eternal Self, the ultimate seer. Pranidhanad refers to the perfect aligning of our being with Ishvara. By adopting the view point of Ishvara as the eternal Self and the pure witness of all experience, our being merges with the vast ocean of the infinite consciousness. This alone can bring higher samadhi quickly into our being.

> 24. *Ishvara, which is untouched by karma, is distinguishable from the root obstructions of consciousness that cause pain.*
> 25. *In Ishvara, the seed of omniscience is unsurpassed.*
> 26. *Ishvara, which is not limited by time or space, is the teacher of even the ancients.*

Ishvara is free of conditioning. By perfect resonance with this principle of creation, the yogi experiences an unconditioned state of consciousness, which is the threshold to full absorption in total liberation and pure being. All time and all places are encompassed in Ishvara as the lord of the universe. By aligning with the principle of Ishvara the yogi learns and grows by the same power that lead the ancient teachers to the realization of the eternal Self.

27. The inner sound current (OM) is the expression of Ishvara.

Permeating all creation is the constant hum of OM. When a yogi, is internalized a sound can be heard within the inner ear and around the head. It may sound like a high-pitched squeal or a constant droning buzz. By directing attention to this sound a yogi can follow it to the source of OM.

The initial sound currents heard may simply be experience of the energy within the nervous system. With intention the yogi listens to the sound behind the initial sound, always trying to hear beyond the sound heard. With practice the sound will grow fuller until it completely absorbs awareness. When this occurs the yogi is fully absorbed in contemplation of the OM vibration.

28. Repetition of the inner sound current (OM) leads to realization of its meaning.

Continuous chanting of OM or repeated sessions of listening to the inner sound current provides experiential insight into the significance of OM as a river of cosmic forces that leads back to Ishvara.

29. From that comes the realization of an inwardly directed consciousness, and the elimination of obstacles.

The vibration of OM flows from rarefied levels of consciousness. Absorption in this sound directs attention inwards. Followed to the source of its emanation (Ishvara), internal obstacles to the liberation of consciousness are dissolved. External obstacles to living a spontaneous and liberated life are also neutralized, as the external experience is merely a reflection of the internal states of consciousness.

> *30. Obstacles that disrupt the field of consciousness include sickness, density, doubt, carelessness, lethargy, sexual preoccupation, erroneous perceptions, failure to obtain grounding in yoga practice, and instability.*

The reality of consciousness is that of a unified field. The ability to perceive the wholeness of consciousness is disrupted by obstacles that can be avoided. Maintaining awareness of the wholeness of consciousness and the wholeness of life itself requires vigilance.

The body is the vehicle by which each individualized unit of pure consciousness processes and relates to itself in manifestation. When spiritual masters proclaim the body as the temple of spirit they are correct. Within the body is housed the ever serene and pure eternal Self. When the body is imbalanced or diseased the probability of experiencing consciousness without condition is greatly lessened.

Density, doubt, carelessness and lethargy in the mind are signs of excess Tamas. The path of Yoga is initially one of moving towards greater clarity and a Sattvic consciousness. A tamasic mind needs motivated towards breaking the inertia that causes one to remain bound in the wheels of karma. This is accomplished by expanding the mind through meditation, cultivating faith in the ability to evolve and grow, being responsible for actions and thoughts, maintaining alert awareness during meditation, and committing to a life enhancing daily routine.

The practice of Yoga requires mental energy to direct attention to a particular truth or technique. Control of the mind is very important in this regard. When the mind can be controlled and all unnecessary thoughts removed or ignored, the remaining energy can be directed to Yoga meditation. Mental preoccupation with sex can greatly distract energy from Yoga. Not only does it disperse the powers of the mind, it also agitates the nervous system thereby dispersing the energy of the body. This makes meditation difficult and lessens the potential for Samadhi.

Erroneous perceptions usually occur as fantasies or half-truths. Devotional meditators may have a tendency to experience visions, which they may mistake as divine revelation or visits of sages or enlightened beings. Half-truths may arise through partial understanding and filling in the rest with imagination. When fantasies are avoided and half-truths are thoroughly researched until the total truth dawns it is easier to remain fully aware of the totality of being. There is nothing other than the yogi, and all knowledge resides within the heart of Pure Being. The yogi is infinitely vaster than a personality or ego viewpoint.

A person unable to firmly establish a Yogic lifestyle is prone to many obstacles to experiencing the wholeness of consciousness. Yoga practice anchors the personality in the eternal Self. In time the personality is seen for what it is, a perspective for the spirit to function in its creation.

When all aspects of the yogi's being is dedicated to realizing the eternal Self true stability manifests. A stable foundation in Yoga and the ability to commit to wholesome lifestyle choices insures rapid progress on the spiritual path.

> *31. These obstacles disrupt the consciousness with pain, depression, restlessness of the body, inhalation and exhalation.*
> *32. The obstacles are prevented by practice of a single truth.*

Disrupting the free flow of consciousness manifests as symptoms of pain, depression and restlessness. When these three characteristics are experienced in the body or mind it is a good time to evaluate what thoughts or actions have arisen to disrupt consciousness. The mind and body are the tools of consciousness. Abusing the tools distorts the ability to realize the wholeness of reality.

Often times Samadhi occurs in a breathless state. This does not mean that the breathing stops altogether, although it may. It indicates that the breath is calm and barely noticeable. When the body or mind is excited or in a state of stress the breathing becomes erratic. Using breathing exercises the breath can be controlled. Once regularity is established the breath can be ignored as meditation progresses. As meditation deepens, the movement of inhalation and exhalation will become barely noticeable.

When the mind is directed to focus on a single truth all other distractions fall away. This is not a suppression of thoughts. This is merely a full absorption in a principle so that everything else falls away. For example, when a person is in a noisy restaurant but engaged in a conversation that absorbs all of their attention they are aware of nothing else. The world is still buzzing all around, but the person hardly notices.

In meditation the yogi can pick a principle such as "I am the infinite consciousness" or "I am peace" or simply "I am" and contemplate with alert attention what that means. The mind is then engaged in discovering the experience of the truth and is not concerned with distracting mental influences.

> 33. The field of consciousness is clarified by a welcoming attitude towards objects of happiness, the demonstration of compassion where there is pain, elation with virtue, and neutrality towards negativity, or non-virtue.

Objects and circumstances that are pleasant maintain optimism and feelings of happiness. There is no need to discard these. Happiness and optimism can contribute to a peaceful mind and a healthy body.

The world contains a polarity that provides experiences of pleasure and pain. When a painful experience occurs to another, a caring attitude can help that person deal appropriately with experience. Compassion is a way of caring without getting caught up in the drama of the situation. By showing compassion where necessary the yogi helps uplift the wholeness of consciousness in which his personality and body abide.

Virtue is that which supports the natural evolution of consciousness. Promoting virtue in the yogi's own life provides a proper demonstration for others to witness the positive experience of living a virtuous life. Virtue also plays a role in avoiding experiences that may be painful and disturb the consciousness. Where there is virtue there is no need for worrying or second-guessing the results of performed actions.

Negativity in the sense of spiritual ignorance arises when a person does not act in a way that promotes their highest good and the realization of the soul nature. Resisting negativity sometimes has the effect of strengthening it. The practice of neutrality in the presence of negativity diffuses the destructive energy and allows it to return to its original potential. From there it can be directed in a positive manner.

> 34. *The field of consciousness can also be clarified by the holding in or out of the breath.*
> 35. *By holding the mind steady on a sensory object consciousness is clarified.*
> 36. *By sorrowless and luminous cognitions consciousness is clarified.*

During Yogic meditation various experiences occur. As the mind becomes calm and still patterns of breathing become subtler. At times the breathing may seem to stop altogether. In Yogic theory it is said that the mind and breath are intimately linked together. When the breath stops so does thinking. During these gaps in thought it is easier to experience the field of the eternal Self. No effort is needed in this regard. By simply being aware in the absence of thought processes invites the realization of the eternal Self to occur. Also note that the breathing is never forced to stop. The breathing stops of its own accord when deep relaxation and mental calm are sustained in meditation.

Fixing the mind on an external object provides a similar effect as mentioned in sutra 32. By directing the full attention to a candle flame, sound, tree, or any other sensory object the mind is restrained. Through this method of restraint the mind becomes able to focus and disregard unnecessary thought patterns that ordinarily cloud awareness and blur the one unified reality of life. The key is providing full attention. It is easy to imagine that the attention is totally engaged in an object of perception while thoughts continue to churn in the background.

When the senses are internalized and the mind is free of thought in meditation inner lights may be perceived in the gaze of the spiritual eye. Some say these lights are the reflection of the life force flowing at the medulla oblongata center. Others note that this may be stimulation of various centers of the brain. Whatever the truth is doesn't matter in this regard. What matters is that these inner lights can be used to further deepen internalized awareness by providing a pleasant object of attention.

When and if the lights are perceived the yogi gives full attention to them. Then attempts can be made to see more deeply into the light. By gazing into the light and attempting to pierce the light with the inner gaze the yogi can follow the light into a samadhi experience.

In Yogic theory the light in the spiritual eye is similar to the light seen at the moment of death. By meditating on this light the yogi consciously, and while still embodied, follows the path taken after death. The practice of penetrating the spiritual eye, with or without lights, eliminates fear of death and provides subtle insights into relationship between life and death. There is an advanced Kriya Yoga technique called Yoni Mudra (sometimes referred to as Jyoti Mudra), which involves a method of piercing the spiritual eye. Yoni is a Sanskrit word referring to the canal through which a person is born. Meditation through the spiritual eye provides a spiritual rebirth to the practitioner.

> *37. Also, by the transcendence of attachment is the field of consciousness cleared.*

The mind has a tendency to cling to experiences. Attachment to experiences creates a duality. When one experience is desired or undesired, categories are created in consciousness that apparently divides the one reality. Release of attachment frees awareness to experience the wholeness of life. Awareness that is unified perceives the truth of reality accurately.

> *38. Also, the field of consciousness is clarified by knowledge of dreams or sleep.*

Recall from sutra 10 that sleep can modify or define awareness. This only occurs when the physical response of sleep fully engages attention so that we are forgetful of our true nature as the witness. By remaining alert and aware of the processes that occur in the mental field during sleep there is no fragmentation in consciousness. Asleep, dreaming, or awake, by maintaining vigilant awareness as the witnessing consciousness at all times the field of consciousness becomes clearer.

39. The field of consciousness is clarified by meditation on one chosen object.

Any object that can fully engage our attention is of value in meditation. Presenting an object to the senses or an idea in the mind and holding firm to contemplation of that object discards all other thoughts. Useful objects may include a candle flame, the sky, or a body of water. If none are present, the eyes can be closed and powers of visualization utilized. Steady contemplation on one single object leaves no room for useless compulsive thinking that clouds awareness. When the thinking process is calm awareness has less obstacles to the experience of pure being that is the eternal Self.

40. Proficient practice of meditation enables mastery of attention and the ability to perceive the smallest and greatest of magnitudes.

There is no separation between one aspect of consciousness and another, just as the wholeness of life, from the smallest atomic particle to the largest galaxy are all an inseparable continuum. Through mastery of attention awareness can be directed to experience any level of consciousness.

41. When the fluctuations in the field of consciousness have diminished, consciousness possesses the clarity of a perfect gemstone. Cognitive blending of the one who experiences, the experience and the experienced occurs.

Normal fragmented awareness divides experience. There is typically the understanding that "I am separate from the objects of my experience." In reality there is no separation. Separation is an illusion. When the fluctuations in consciousness cease a person knows that the individualized perspective is one with the objects of their perception as well as that which makes possible the experience.

Before the understanding of wholeness spontaneously emerges in awareness, it is helpful to imagine what it would be like if this were the current experience of reality.

42. Cognitive blending may occur while the thinking process of knowledge and conceptualization still functions.

Thinking about the world and placing labels on circumstances can still occur when awareness shifts from the limited ego to the witnessing consciousness of the eternal Self. Then we are aware of even the thinking processes and the ego as part of the one whole eternal Self, which extends from the field of pure consciousness all the way to the material world uninterrupted.

43. When the cognitive blending is further purified there is only the experience of the field of consciousness shining as its own object.

As over identification with the thinking and conceptualizing process is neutralized, the eternal Self shines through everything as one undivided consciousness. Then all that exists in awareness is realized to be one thing, consciousness.

44. *Both forms of cognitive blending give knowledge of subtle realms.*

Both experiences of cognitive blending provides direct insight into states of consciousness not normally accessible to human awareness. Cognitive blending as it is spoken of in these sutras refers to a superconscious state. In superconsciousness subtler functions of the one reality are more easily understood. For example, the knowledge and understanding of cosmic manifestation outlined in the Samkhya philosophy emerges innately from this state. The realization of outer circumstances manifesting as a reflection of internal states of consciousness is more easily recognized.

45. *These subtle realms extend to the primary unmanifest state of matter.*

While functioning in superconscious meditation the yogi can explore states of consciousness all the way back to ground of being, the field from which all creation springs.

46. *These are lower forms of Samadhi with support.*

Full absorption in a state of consciousness is considered a lower samadhi. A "state of consciousness" can be an object of attention. When there is an object of attention that leads to Samadhi it is said to be supported state of one-ness. The yogi experiences oneness with a "thing." A state of consciousness may not be considered a "thing" by most people because of its subtlety, but anything that can be witnessed is transient.

47. *The realization of the eternal Self occurs through reflection without support.*

Samadhi without a support is the higher Samadhi. When there is no support there is only full abidance in the eternal Self, which is unmodified and unconditioned. It cannot be seen, touched, or experienced. It can only be what it is.

48. *In this state, insight bears truth.*

Absorbed fully in the eternal Self, all that needs to be known is revealed. Here, knowledge of the oneness consciousness is perfect.

49. *The truth then comes from a deeper level than anything heard or inferred.*

The flawless truth revealed through uniting attention with the eternal Self surpasses anything imaginable. It is beyond the mind, the word, and experience. It cannot be described.

50. *The conditioning born of that insight neutralizes truth veiling conditioning of the normal human state.*

Awareness that is united with the eternal Self purifies all definitions that blur and fragment consciousness, thereby giving rise to the normal human condition. Repeated episodes of Samadhi (higher and lower) frees the eternal Self to experience the truth of its own nature without the confusion of imagining that it is a limited individualized ego. Every time awareness is immersed in Samadhi the eternal Self is freed to experience the wholeness of life without limitation.

> *51. When that insight ends all conditioning, then higher samadhi is experienced without support.*

When no more conditioning remains to blur and fragment awareness, the eternal Self is free to express in all conditions. Here the yogi experiences the eternal Self as everything with no separation from the wholeness of life and no chance of falling back into delusion. This is the higher Samadhi that is every person's natural state as a spiritual being temporarily relating to a human condition.

Through the diligent, and consistent application of yogic methods, this is realized without a doubt.

Chapter 6

SPIRITUAL PRACTICE

Part 2: The Chapter on Spiritual Practice

1. Kriya Yoga is intensity in spiritual practice; learning and application of one's own Self-study, and the perfect alignment of attention with Ishvara.

Kriya Yoga is a process of living that allows the spontaneous emergence of higher knowledge from the core of being. A Kriya is a cleansing action that removes obstacles to the self shining awareness of experiencing one's own true nature.

Advanced pranayama techniques, taught through the lineage of gurus beginning with Babaji and Lahiri Mahasaya, are often considered to be the practice of Kriya Yoga, as they cleanse the mind/body unit of conditioning that normally limits the expression of Self-Realized qualities. This is a common misunderstanding. This idea does not reveal the full scope of the practice. In reality, any action that clarifies awareness for the emergence of Self-Realization can be considered Kriya Yoga.

Spiritual practice involves any authentic method that is employed to expand consciousness and invite the flow of grace from the practitioners concept of the divine. This can include mantra, prayer, chanting, meditation, service performed for the benefit of all, etc.

Self-study is necessary to understand the purpose of life, thereby promoting living in accord with dharma. According to the Bhagavad-Gita, "Better is one's own duty [dharma] though imperfectly performed than the duty of another performed well. Better is defeat in one's own duty, for to follow another's path is to invite difficulty." When one knows one's purpose in life, it can be performed as spiritual practice. Then even the very act of living becomes sacred service. On a deeper level, Self-study also provides insight into the ultimate purpose of life, which is the reason everyone is here. It provides knowledge of the eternal Self behind the transient mind and personality. This is also understood to be "Self-inquiry".

The purpose of aligning attention with Ishvara was mentioned in the first section of the sutras. Ishvara, representing the pure state of being, quickly frees consciousness from delusion when the yogi experiences the life situation as a direct expression of that being.

2. *It has the purpose of realizing samadhi and dissolving the root causes of pain.*

Dedicated Kriya Yoga practice removes all obstacles to the realization of samadhi, oneness consciousness. As consciousness is clarified the painful experiences common to the average human condition are eliminated from the possibility of expressing. This state is sometimes referred to as enlightenment, but is really the natural state of all people at the deepest level of their existence. Those who comprehend the usefulness of Kriya Yoga and know the possibility of such soul freedom can quickly awaken to re-alization of the wholeness of life.

3. *Absence of Self-awareness, a sense of individual-ized existence apart from the wholeness of life, at-tachment, aversion and the will to live are the root causes of pain.*

Absence of Self-awareness is ignorance. When the awareness of the Self is confused or absent, choices are made and actions performed that may not be for the high-est good. Through Self-awareness, the relationship be-tween effective life enhancing actions and states of con-sciousness are easily discerned. A Self-aware person functions easily and effectively in the world.

Normal human consciousness errs in imagining that there is a separation between the Self and the surround-ings. This causes pain by distorting the truth. What af-fects one person affects everybody, or what affects the en-vironment also affects the Self, because they are not sepa-rate.

Attachment and aversion are two sides of the same coin. Through attachment comes a need to re-experience a past sensation. This longing causes pain. Aversion creates a state of anxiety about re-experiencing a past pain. Both aversion and attachment create dissonance by projecting the idea that peace exists through gaining something or avoiding something. The nature of phenomenal existence is change. The cycles of pleasure and pain continue until awareness goes beyond them. By accepting the present moment in whatever form it presents itself, attachment and aversion cease. Then the eternal Self shines through everything clearly.

Life is everything. It is the perpetual movement of consciousness and the energy behind all forms. It is indestructible. Pain arises when the notion of an end to life is imagined. In this sutra "clinging to life", which is inferred, refers to the inertia of the tendencies of the current incarnation.

4. *Absence of self-awareness is the field for the other root causes of pain. They can be dormant, weak, restrained or active.*

Ignorance is the ground from which the seeds of pain grow. Through Kriya Yoga ignorance is dissolved in the light of Self-awareness. Kriya Pranayama is said to roast the seeds of karma before they can sprout. As one's karma becomes less, one's ability to see clearly is increased. Self-awareness destroys dormant pain before it can express. Causes of pain which are said to be "weakly expressing" can be further weakened and destroyed. The potential for pain that is attempting to express or is fully expressive is neutralized as Self-awareness grows. Dedicated living of the Kriya Yoga philosophy and practice of the advanced pranayama techniques, clears out the sub-conscious and makes peaceful the observable conscious-ness.

> 5. *Absence of self-awareness arises from imagining the impermanent to be permanent, the impure to be pure, pain to be happiness, and the non-self to be the Self.*

When life is appreciated at a superficial level the transient rise and fall of names and forms appears to be the permanent reality. All that appears disappears. There is a source to this superficial play of light and shade that is pure, eternal and changeless. Inquiring to know what it is like to be that level of existence produces Self-awareness.

The senses carry experience to our witnessing conscious-ness. What delights the senses may not necessarily promote the highest good if discrimination and Self-knowledge are lacking. Enjoyment of the senses simply for the sake of preventing boredom may provide immediate, although passing, happiness. Turning attention inward and following the senses back to their source provides insight into the nature of the senses. Gaining insight, one sees the error in catering to immediate sense gratification in exchange for delighting in the permanent reality of peace that results from disciplined spiritual practice.

Just as the changing face of the one reality can be imagined to *be* the one reality, a person's personality, mind and ego is often imagined to *be* the true Self. Pain is avoided by knowing the changeless Self rather than identifying with the transient self.

> *6. Individualized awareness is identification of the two distinct powers of seeing and what is seen.*

The power to see and the object seen are not two distinct things. Both are aspects of consciousness. Consciousness is not divided on any level. When the idea arises that there is a division in consciousness so does a sense of individualized awareness.

At first the yogi may lack the insight to comprehend everything as an undivided aspect of the eternal Self. When this is the case it is useful to spend time discriminating between anything that can be experienced and the witnessing consciousness. The yogi is to know that the untouchable witnessing consciousness cannot be seen; it can only be what it is. People, places, sounds, memories, thoughts, emotions, visions, fantasies, dreams or any other phenomena are objects to be witnessed and are not the eternal Self, the witnessing consciousness. Once stable in the realization of the witnessing consciousness the yogi can then inquire into how all manifesting existence is an expression of the yogi's consciousness and thereby an undivided aspect of that consciousness. Then insight into this sutra will be revealed from within. Dawning of this insight may take time and consistent contemplation.

> *7. Attachment is holding on to previous happiness.*

Happiness that no longer exists is just a memory with no real object in the present. Longing for past objects that created a pleasant mood is attachment. It is also a denial of the present moment, which is all there ever is. Attachment destroys the sacredness of life by denying life. Life is not in the past or the future. It is in the eternal present. Maintaining awareness in the present relieves the soul of the bonds of attachment.

8. *Aversion is holding on to previous pain.*

When the mind has been conditioned to associate pain with a circumstance it seeks to avoid reliving that circumstance. This is useful to a degree, as it helps avoid common sense errors, such as burning the hand on a stove, or avoiding bad relationships. Trouble arises when the aversion becomes neurotic such as in the instance of avoiding relationships due to past heart ache and loss.

There is always opportunity for change in life. If certain circumstances repeat frequently it is more useful to explore belief and thought patterns that might need discovered and altered to end a cycle of painful experiences. Preoccupation with past pain is not useful in the present where it no longer exists. Habitual mental tendencies that need to be changed to live a peaceful and fulfilled life can be altered through consistent acts of will.

9. *The will to live is compelling, even in the wise.*

Even spiritual masters may briefly experience this pain when it comes time for their transition. This can be likened to a wild bird that has been caged too long and then given the opportunity to be free. It may have grown comfortable in the cage and fear the return to freedom. As it has been said before, the eternal Self is the bird and the body and personality the cage. On a subtle level, this can also influence daily meditation practice. If we are afraid to let go of our false sense of self, we will have difficulty experiencing the Absolute.

> *10. Those subtle root causes of pain that are not yet active are to be ended by returning them to their source.*

The Eternal Self is the source of all objects, experiences and circumstances. Consciousness becomes confused when it identifies with the transient creation and forgets about the changeless reality of the eternal Self. It is this confusion about the true nature of the Self that causes pain.

Looking on and witnessing the arising of the root causes of pain in the field of consciousness destroys them. By watching the root cause of pain as a detached witness the divine presence looks on through the individualized awareness and dissolves the causes.

> *11. Definitions of the field of consciousness arising from the root causes of pain are to be ended through meditation.*

Meditation brings stillness to the mind. A still mind allows being to express flawlessly. Alert attention maintained in a field of pure being allows Self-awareness to flow forth easily. Where there is Self-awareness there are no root causes of pain. Where there are no root causes of pain, there are no definitions of consciousness. Then the Eternal self is experienced and appreciated fully as one pure undivided consciousness. That is what we are at the absolute level of existence.

> *12. Having its origin in the root causes of pain the accumulation of karma can be experienced in births, seen and unseen.*

Karma manifests by way of the root causes of pain. The more often they are allowed to express the greater the karmic load that accumulates. The seeds of karma have three main states: expressed, expressing or dormant.

Karma that has already been experienced can be released. It doesn't matter what a person has or hasn't done in the past. What matters is their current resolve to change what needs changing and live an effective Self-Aware life in the present. Karma that is expressing can be ended by making a conscious decision to end the circumstances. If there is nothing that can be done to end it, then patiently wait for it to pass. Letting go of past karma and neutralizing present karmic tendencies is a sure way to destroy dormant karma before it can manifest.

Experiences and states of consciousness are a continuous reflection of choices that have been and are currently being made. Coming to terms with the past and doing what a person knows to be best is the most efficient way to neutralize karma, seen or unseen.

> *13. As long as there is an origin of karma, birth, life and life experiences will ripen and express.*

As long as Self-awareness is absent the seeds of karma will continue to have fertile ground in which to grow. The average human condition consists of unconscious involvement with physical birth, situations that occur after birth, and termination of the body. Average human consciousness, which is fragmented, experiences pain due to this seemingly uncontrollable series of events.

With the emergence of Self-awareness comes the realization of what life truly is in relation to the whole of which it is a part. With Self-awareness the origins of karma are destroyed. When a fragmented consciousness is clarified and united with its infinite wholeness, which it has always been, the expression of karma grows weaker until it is totally non-influential. Then consciousness expresses freely without compulsion. Then there is no birth, life or death. There is only the eternal existence of what is, forever in the eternal pure consciousness.

> *14. These births express distress or delight depending on the virtuous or non virtuous nature of their origin.*

The term birth will be taken to refer simply to the arising of new events in a life situation.

Events occur because of preexisting conditions and circumstances that give them birth. The quality of the event is dependant on the energy put into and preceding the event. Many lives are marked by a continuous pattern of repetitive circumstances. Some people may experience a particular situation many times in life while others never will. This occurs because situations are sustained by a state of consciousness that supports and invites them.

If the life is to be changed, so must the habitual state of consciousness. If life is unpleasant or not supportive of expressing Self awareness, then thoughts, actions and feelings that maintain this situation will need to be discovered and dissolved if change is desired. Then mental shifts and outward actions directed to manifesting a positive uplifting life experience can be applied to insure a positive and uplifting experience in the new vision of the present and future.

> *15. Because of suffering arising from subconscious subliminal tendencies that cause changes and fluctuations due to the primal forces of nature, to one with discrimination, all is pain.*

The Gunas, here referred to as the primal forces of nature, are constantly in an interplay of change. For a time each Guna dominates in expression keeping an unequal proportion in the influence of the other two. When the Gunas are equalized creation dissolves back into the source of its origin. Why and how this occurs is covered in the fourth portion of Patanjali's sutras.

The Gunas influence all levels of creation, from cosmic cycles all the way to the mental genetics of a human individual. Their activity creates and stimulates impulses in the subconscious mind of the individual and also in the Cosmic Mind of the universe. These impulses provide the seeds of experience. As they grow from the subconscious level of being, they eventually emerge into an experiential reality for the being to which they belong.

Identification with the changing tides of the Guna influences causes pain through the experience of loss. The nature of change creates and destroys. When attached to an expression that is bound to dissolve, pain is always somehow experienced.

16. Suffering not yet experienced is to be ended.
17. What is to be ended is the correlation between the seer with the seeable.
18. The seeable has the characteristics of luminosity (Sattva), activity (Rajas), and inertia (Tamas). It is embodied in the elements and the sense organs. It exists for experience and emancipation.

Knowing the source of suffering, it is appropriate to take the necessary steps to put an end to it. A healthy minded individual does not enjoy suffering.

All that can be witnessed in any way is transient. The eternal Self can never be witnessed. It is not a series of thoughts, sense experiences, state of consciousness or anything else that can be described. It is the experiencer of all these. Imagining the seer to be what it is not, is the source of pain.

The characteristics of what can be seen are supported by the luminosity of Sattva, the active and dissipating action of Rajas, and the stabilizing inertia of Tamas. Through the elements of nature and organs that convey sensation to the mind, the seeable exists for experience and eventually the final liberation of the witnessing consciousness from identification with what it is not.

19. The phases of the primal forces of creation are visible, atomic, the manifest, and the unmanifest (prakriti).

The interplay of the primal forces of creation (the Gunas) gives rise to four modes of expression. The visible includes the gross elemental substances of ether, air, fire, water and earth. On subtler level these relate to the five sense organs that perceive the elements, the motor organs that act upon the elements, and the mind, which reflects the process to the eternal Self.

The atomic includes the qualities of the senses that give rise to the elements: sound, touch, sight, taste, and smell. The atomic also includes the sense of individualized existence.

The visible and atomic expressions are the product of the manifest principle of creation. This is the cosmic mind that is made up of all individual minds. The manifest in relationship to this sutra relates to the innate intelligence of creation.

Prakriti holds all potentials for expression. She is the field of all potentials, the ground of being, and the source for all previous expressions mentioned here. Just thinking about or analyzing this concept may not be very helpful. Remember that it often takes consistent and intensive contemplation over time before understanding of more esoteric principles are fully realized.

20. The seer is the act of seeing alone. It is pure even when witnessing thoughts directed to an object.

A person established in total Self-awareness embodies purity. Thoughts and experiences can still arise in the field of awareness for one established in Self-awareness. With the dawning of total Self-awareness comes the realization of being what one has always been at the deepest level of being, a witness to every passing phenomenon.

The idea of seeing encompasses all the senses, so it may make more sense to think of the seer as the experiencer. When consciousness is only aware of experiencing it is whole. In the act of experiencing there is only what is. The need to label and conceptualize the experience is unnecessary. Some may argue that the act of thinking about an experience is equally part of the experience. They fail to realize that an experience can only be thought about after it passes. Trying to think about something as it occurs is impossible. There is always a fraction of time when the experience has to simply happen while being absorbed by the senses before being relayed to the mind.

When a person is continually trying to or compulsively thinking about all experiences as they arise the experience is missed altogether. Instead, the actual experience is replaced by the mental noise of the mind impatiently trying to label and judge the moment the experience occurs. In this situation the person is missing the reality and instead only experiencing the mental whine of a mind that is out of control.

The mind isn't all that important when it comes to the experience of being. It is important for balancing a checkbook or communicating with words, but how does it enrich the experience of a soul that is beyond the limit of concepts and thoughts? How does it enrich the experience of a sunset by trying to remember the different kinds of clouds reflecting the golden glow? Being with the sunset unlocks the spirit and oneness in the experience. Later on words can help share the experience with another.

The act of seeing alone uncovers the eternal Self. Thinking is a tool like any other. It is just as useless to think constantly out of compulsion as it is to refuse to put down a hammer that has already served its purpose.

21. The seeable is only for the purpose of the seer.

It has already been stated in sutra 18 that the seeable exists for "experience and emancipation." All that exists does so for the benefit of the Eternal self. Consciousness being infinite possesses an infinite potential for learning and growth. When a portion of the infinite consciousness develops an individualized sense of self and falls into deluded identification with mind and matter another round of evolution begins.

The eternal Self remains what it ever has been; yet it undergoes identification with phenomena to experience evolution into a more stable state of realization. Through the process of experience and emancipation the eternal Self fully banishes the tendency towards forgetfulness.

22. When the seers purpose is complete the seeable ceases. It also has not ceased since it is common to others.

The purpose of the seer is total liberation of consciousness. When this occurs the world of form, as it was known before complete liberation of consciousness, no longer exists. Yet it does still exist for those individualized units of consciousness that have not yet completed the process of liberation.

Various life situations express in different ways depending on the needed growth of the experiencer. One person may experience the same life lesson repeatedly and wonder why the experience never changes or why that same situation hardly ever occurs in the life of others they know. When the purpose of the life lesson is learned and the person moves on, the experience will cease to occur. Yet, it may still occur for others who have not yet learned the lesson.

The ultimate purpose of the soul is to merge back into the unconditioned pure consciousness. All experiences are presented for that one purpose. When the purpose is complete, the presentation of experiences stops.

23. The correlation between the seer and the seeable is the cause of perception of the powers of the Self and the domain in which it functions.

The correlation between the seer and seeable is an error of perception. This causes the false imagination that the Self and the world of experience are essentially separate. The Self is thought of as "in here" and the world of experience is thought of as "out there". When awareness is clear, the inseparable nature of the Self and the world of experience is realized. The Self is just as much "in here" as "out there. The same holds true of the world of experience. Both concepts are two sides of the same coin.

24. *The cause of that correlation is the absence of Self-Awareness.*
25. *Owing to the disappearance of ignorance there is the ending of the correlation between the seer and the seen. That is the aloneness of seeing.*

Ignorance of the true nature of the Self is the prime cause of this correlation. As the veil of ignorance dissolves the threads that maintain the correlation between the seer and the seen unravels. Then there is no seer and no seen. There simply is the act of seeing. Here duality is no longer entertained. There is only existence-being, free of all conditioned states.

26. *Unceasing discrimination between the seer and the seen is the way to ending the correlation.*

The commentary on sutra 23 may seem to contradict the message in sutra 26. The contradiction is only superficial, yet necessary for the instruction of those still suffering from absence of Self-awareness.

Before a truth seeker can fully embrace the seamless infinite expression of consciousness, from the purest consciousness free of all conditioning to the grossest levels of form, unyielding discrimination between the witnessing presence and the objects to be witnessed is necessary. This has the effect of freeing the awareness from identifying with limited states of consciousness. When the thought arises that I am "this" or "that", consciousness becomes limited to that expression of its self.

In V.72 of Vasistha's Yoga, Vasistha explains to Rama:

"The self is neither this nor that; it transcends whatever is the object of experiencing here. In the unlimited and unconditioned vision of the knower of truth, all this is but the one Self, the infinite consciousness, and there is nothing that can be regarded as the not-self. The substantiality of all substances is none other than the Self or the infinite consciousness."

Before the complete realization of being the infinite consciousness, the truth seeker must first be totally free of all conditioning. That is the purpose of discrimination between the seer and the seen.

27. The way to this insight culminates in seven stages.

Self-realization develops through seven successive stages. Each stage represents a refining of consciousness until consciousness is completely at peace within its own being.

At the first stage the impulse towards Self-realization emerges. Ordinary fragmented consciousness is recognized for what it is, and the desire to be free from it is evident. Self-defeating habits are discerned and the action to resolve them is the main focus. Spiritual practice may be undertaken to calm the mind and gain mastery of attention.

During the second stage behavior and thinking are now constructive. If there are still negative traits, they are few and easily overcome by an act of will. At this stage a person is well adjusted and functions easily within the world without undue stress. During meditation practice the attention is easily concentrated on the object of contemplation.

Superconsciousness prevails at the third stage. The mind has been calmed and attention is easily directed to a single source. The life is well ordered and the comprehension of what needs to be done to awaken to full liberation of consciousness is easily understood. Spiritual practices performed at this stage are capable of providing insight into subtler states of consciousness.

At the fourth stage the wholeness of life is easily discerned. A person experiences the connection between the eternal Self, the mind, and internal and external states of consciousness. The mind is understood as a tool for the expression of the eternal Self, and not mistaken as the definition of what a person is. At this level of development the reflection of external circumstances is understood to be an effect of internal states of consciousness.

The fifth stage is marked by complete control of the mind and emotions. Random thoughts and uncontrollable emotions no longer disturb the realization of being one's own eternal Self. The mind is used when it is needed and no longer incessantly intrudes on the act of remaining as the witnessing consciousness.

Uncompromising identification with the eternal Self is evident at the sixth stage. Not even the primal forces of nature can disturb the witnessing consciousness. Here a person understands their reality as an individualized yet fully integrated unit of the one field of consciousness.

The seventh stage is not describable with words. All that can be said is that the eternal Self is supremely free. All subtle restrictions to the realization of existence as pure infinite being are non-existent for one abiding at this level of realization. All that needs to be accomplished is finished. The purpose of the universe is realized completely for one at this stage.

Many spiritual aspirants try to skip the first two stages, thinking that they are not important. It is stages one and two that creates the foundation for the rest of the process. Just as a building needs a solid structure beneath it to stand strong, so do our endeavors need a solid foundation if our efforts towards Self-realization are going to mature.

It will be noticed that individuals are more likely to have authentic sustained awakening experiences when they live an orderly life and take responsibility for their own well being and those in their care.

> 28. By practicing the eight limbs of yoga, as the impurities diminish, there is a light of knowing leading to discrimination.

Complete practice of yoga, of which there are eight aspects, removes the impurities that block realization of spiritual freedom. First, the impurities are removed. As these impurities dissolve our powers of discrimination develop. Discrimination is invaluable to fully comprehend the knowledge that unfolds from within us to impart our total spiritual freedom.

Knowledge of the eternal Self is compared to light in this sutra. As the particles of ignorance are wiped away from the spotlight of divine grace through dedicated yoga practice, the light of knowing shines forth freely. Then we are in the flow of spiritual realization. The flow never responds to force, but it will flow when obstacles to its path are removed.

> 29. *Yama, niyama, asana, pranayama, pratyahara, dharana, dhyana, and samadhi are the eight limbs.*

The eight aspects to be practiced are: refraining from harmful behaviors, cultivating life-enhancing behaviors, developing steady meditation posture, practice of scientific breathing techniques, inward flowing of attention from the senses, focused attention, meditation, and cognitive absorption.

> 30. *Non violence, truth, non stealing, conservation of vital forces, and non possessiveness are the yamas-universal disciplines.*

The universal disciplines outline behaviors and states of mind conducive to soul peace. For the peace of the eternal Self to manifest fully, a foundation in the universal disciplines is essential.

> 31. *The universal disciplines are applicable irrespective of one's state of life, place, time, or circumstance.*

Many people imagine that things will be different after they die. Either they will be rewarded with an afterlife of eternal bliss or they will be roasting their toes in lakes of fire because of their past sins. This may be true for those with a powerful enough imagination to sustain such a state, but for the knower of reality the future is no different than the present. Neither death nor any other modification of the environment will do much to make a permanent change in the current experiences of the knower.

Death is often likened to casting off used garments. The body falls and the soul carries on. Keeping this in mind, remember the last time you changed your clothes. Was your body radically different from the change? Did your basic views on life change? No they did not. Changes to the body and mind structure only occur through effort. The same is true about one's general experience in life.

Remember that life is eternal. Life is not bound by birth or death. Birth and death are the two polarities in which life is temporarily confined for an incarnation. Before birth, life is the same. After death, life is still the same. The quality of life can be improved through living in harmony with the natural laws of the universe. If living in this way is not natural in the present moment this may take intention and commitment. Otherwise, inertia will carry the force of the present onwards without change.

All of this is important to know in regard to the yamas, because our spiritual development is not confined to this single personality experience we are currently aware of. It spans great ages of existence-being. The yamas are the foundation for spiritual practice and function as proper support no matter what our current experience, incarnate or otherwise. As the march of time moves on so does life continue to interact with the manifest creation. This may take numerous and varied forms, but no matter the place, state, time or circumstance actualization of the yamas ensures harmonious interactions and accelerated spiritual growth.

32. *Purity, contentment, intensity in spiritual practice, practice of learned personal mantras, and alignment of attention with the Eternal Self—the witnessing consciousness—are the internal disciplines, the niyamas.*

The niyamas are internal disciplines that make the practice of the yamas easier. Together the yamas and niyamas create a mental framework enabling proper interaction with the world so that the personal and universal purpose of life is assured.

33. *Upon elimination of opposing beliefs, there is the experience of their opposites.*
34. *Beliefs [at odds with yoga] such as violence result in pain and ignorance. These beliefs are upheld through direct action, the seeds of action, and the approval of action. They can be mild, moderate, or excessive in degree. When resolved through meditation on the results of these beliefs, their opposites prevail.*

The world in which we live is responsive to our states of being. Whatever is within us will be reflected in our experiences. Inner states of fear, violence, or any other destructive tendency need to be eliminated through cultivation of their opposites.

States of consciousness that sustain pain in the life experience and ignorance of the eternal Self are at odds with the practice of Yoga. Through inner reflection we can become aware of the existence of these states within our self. We can then grasp how they are upheld through our own subconscious patterns, the actions we perform in the world, and the approval of these actions performed by others.

When meditating on the results of how maintaining states of ignorance and pain within us affects us and the world, we can then resolve to restrain and neutralize their expression. Then our consciousness naturally becomes lighter, more whole, and more directly attuned with our eternal Self.

35. When one is established in non-violence, violence is relinquished in one's presence.

Violence easily disturbs the mind and life force of the one who commits the action and the one who receives the force of the action. When we refrain from violence we stop reinforcing the tendency to violence in our self and in our environment. Non-violence has many levels. Violence can be committed in thought, speech or action, and can be directed to others or our own self. To be fully established in non-violence requires an awareness of all the ways in which it can occur. Through gentle intention we can identify and root out anything contrary to the discipline of harmlessness.

36. When one is established in truthfulness, the results of actions are assured.

Truth is another factor to promote peace of mind and strength of body, both of which are necessary for proper yoga practice. If we are established in truth we expend less energy trying to maintain a facade, which promotes needless worry and dissipation of our powers of concentration. The body is also weakened by non-truth as is evidenced by the weakening effect on muscles during the verbalization of a lie.

37. When established in non stealing, all prosperity is attained.

When a person engages in stealing, the person affirms a consciousness of lack. This strengthens the tendency to not have enough in life. The One Consciousness responds to our individual states of being. When we steal, we are saying to the universe, "There are not enough resources for me, so I must take it from another." The universe confirms the statement by making it a reality. The cycle continues. We live in an infinite universe with infinite resources. Living from a consciousness of lack denies this fact. By changing the pattern of lack to one of abundance, all is provided for. Stealing is harmful to those taken from as well as to the thief.

38. When all conduct and desires lead to the Eternal Self, one obtains vital energy.

Vital forces represent many kinds of energy. Conservation of these forces in the context of this sutra implies dedication of them to the practice of yoga. Our ultimate purpose on this earth is to realize our Eternal Self. This is the purpose of all of consciousness on an absolute level. When an individualized unit of the one field begins to consciously cooperate with this process, the one field takes great interest. Then, all resources in the infinite universe become available to that purpose. The vital energy obtained is in relation to the degree of harmony with the absolute universal process of Self-realization.

As individualized units of the one field of consciousness we all have unique talents and goals to express. Yoga meditation quickens our awakening. So does expressing our talents and achieving our goals appropriately. By dedicating our meditative practice *and* our actions in life to Self-realization all forms of vital energy are obtained to support the process. This can manifest as health, abundant resources, or even supportive relationships. Whatever is needed is provided.

39. Understanding of why births occur is founded in non-possessiveness.

Possessiveness leads to attachment and aversion. Before the actual realization dawns that all is consciousness and we are all of that, it may be helpful to imagine that happiness and peace are not achieved by the possessions we can gather and hold on to. Neither is it had by acquiring something that appears to make another happy. The down side of possessiveness is the great propensity it can create to disturb the mind. It also creates an inertia towards desiring more and so worrying more in the event of losing what is gained.

Traditionally speaking, the reason births occur is due to the presence of desire in the soul. When there is a desire, the universe creates an opportunity for that desire to be had. If that opportunity requires a new experience to be birthed, then that is what occurs. The yama of non-possessiveness is extolled so that it is easy to relate to objects and people without attachment, and also to end the tedious wheel of rebirth. Contrary to popular belief, we are not here to see how much we can "get into", but to exhaust our desires so that we can direct our attention to what really matters, figuring out who we really are.

40. *By practicing purity, the desire arises to protect one's body from adverse conditions.*

Some desires are necessary for the realization of our ultimate purpose. The desire to protect and maintain the health of the body is supportive of our spiritual endeavors. When the body is strong and vital it is easier to live effectively. There is also less interference in our mental field when our body functions properly. Through proper care of the body we assure that it does not take away attention from our spiritual practices.

41. *Due to purity, the clarity of Sattva manifests inspiration, one pointedness, mastery of the sense organs and readiness for seeing the Eternal Self.*

The original nature of the mind is Sattvic. The mind is meant to function as a clear receptive station for the experiences carried to it through the sense organs. Purity of the body and mind are synergistic. Maintaining a clear mental field relieves stress in the body. A healthy body allows the mind to experience its natural equilibrium. When the body and mind are united in a Sattvic state, the three primary requisites for proper yoga practice manifest. The mind can maintain concentration without distraction. The sense organs are controlled so they can be directed inward. The embodied soul is then prepared to await the experience of the Eternal Self.

42. *When one is content there arises and unexcelled happiness.*

True contentment is not found in the gaining of objects or experiences thought to produce it. This is evidenced through experience. Once an object or experience is acquired, it may please the mind for a little while. Then the mind becomes restless again and seeks more stimulation. True contentment is not dependant on the stimulation of experience. When we have cultivated contentment beyond experiences, a blissfulness emerges that cannot be broken.

43. *Spiritual practice eliminates impurities, and results in perfection of the body and the sense organs.*

The purpose of spiritual practice is to gain mastery over the sense organs and eliminate the impurities that block the ceaseless flow of grace. Grace is always flowing to us throughout the universe. Most people cannot receive this grace because they are distracted by the outward flowing energy of their sense organs. Spiritual practice develops the power of focused attention that allows us to direct our consciousness inward.

When we can sustain our intention to focus on the heart of our being, our eternal Self, healing energy flows are released throughout the body. This allows the body to function properly. We are more inclined to be healthy, to be happy and to live longer. In this way, we have ample time to attend to our mundane and spiritual duties without distraction.

> 44. *Owing to the application of learned personal mantras, one unites with one's concept of the divine. Inspiration arises.*

In the context of these sutras, mantra refers to Sanskrit phrases utilized to invoke the spiritual power of various aspects of the divine. Through the heartfelt repetition of the mantras, a person unites with their own concept of the divine, as it is real to them. The resulting devotional ardor propels them forward on their spiritual path.

Neither Sanskrit mantra nor properly formulated word phrases are necessary for the principle outlined in this sutra to function. Any thought or action that unites awareness with the divine, as it is real to you, will serve the same purpose. Constant remembrance of the reality of God being all things can be sustained in the background of your mind through daily activity. This can be brought to the forefront of your attention during deep meditation. You could even repeat the phrase "I am peace" throughout the day as your personal inspirational mantra. The goal is to inspire your thoughts and actions to realize your true nature as a spiritual being.

Also note that as your understanding grows your concept of the divine will change. This evolution will continue until you flawlessly perceive the true nature of yourself and your relationship with the infinite consciousness.

45. Perfect cognitive absorption results from the perfect aligning of attention with the Eternal Self.

When we are in a state of perfect cognitive absorption there is a total integration of all levels of being. Here there is no dividing boundary between the mind, body and spirit. The quickest way to experience this reality is to give full attention to the eternal Self, the heart of your being.

At first this may be difficult, but each attempt carries you closer to sustaining this realization effortlessly. Many people give up too soon. They try aligning their attention a few times and then throw up their hands saying it is impossible. It is not impossible. It requires persistence and faith. Through persistence we learn to feel out the process and perfect our attempts. Through faith we acknowledge the certainty of the outcome and develop our imagination as a tool for shaping reality.

It may also be useful to remember that you already *are* perfectly aligned with the eternal Self, and that there already *is* no division between the mind, body and spirit. As you endeavor to realize this, keep in mind that your thoughts, emotions, and experiences are all an expression of the eternal Self. The thoughts you think, the emotions you feel, and the experiences you witness are the thoughts, emotions and experiences of the one consciousness. You are the witness of a cosmic process playing out through your own life situation.

46. *Asana is any posture that is stable and comfortable.*

Proper meditation requires an alert yet relaxed body. The spine and head should be erect. The rest of the body needs to be relaxed yet poised.

Tension can be dispersed through deep breathing. By taking two to three deep breaths all tension can be released on exhalation. Imagine the body is held straight by a string at the very top of the head. On each exhale, the muscles of the shoulders, chest and abdomen are allowed to soften. All the while the body is prevented from slouching by the support of the imaginary thread at the top of the head.

An upright sitting posture is recommended because it helps to maintain alert attention. Lying down is not advised, because this triggers the body to sleep. Slouching is also to be avoided, because this stresses the muscles of the back and also leads to semi conscious states, such as daydreaming.

47. *Asana becomes stable and comfortable when effort is relaxed and cognitive processes blend with the infinite consciousness.*

With practice the body becomes stable and comfortable during meditation. Initial bodily distractions, such as itches or not being comfortable, become less prominent.

The more often a person sits to meditate, the quicker the body becomes trained to internalize attention for the purpose of spiritual growth.

It is helpful to be certain of the reason for your meditation practice to aid the process. When you are focused on the purpose of blending your imaginary sense of self as a limited finite being into the one infinite consciousness of which we are all a part, external stimuli are less noticeable.

The idea of relaxing effort in this sutra indicates that one's attitude is free of strain or excessive force. The upright posture, with attention internalized, is maintained by an act of gentle intention.

48. Stable in that posture one experiences freedom from the afflictions of duality—pleasure and pain.

Gaining control of our body enables us to disregard the energy dispersing afflictions of pleasure and pain. Pleasure and pain are the main physical means of conditioning. We seek out experiences that are pleasurable and tenaciously avoid experiences that are unpleasant. Even when not present, the mind whirls with ways to experience the pleasurable and avoid the painful. In both instances the mind can become distracted from the important goal of spiritual realization. Stable in the meditation posture and with the intention to go beyond the duality of pleasure and pain, awareness is released into the infinite consciousness.

49. Once a stable posture or asana is achieved, one can then practice pranayama effectively.

Pranayama is breathing with awareness. A stable body allows one to give their full attention to breathing. Simply observing the breath as it moves in and out of the body, without trying to change it in anyway, is a method of pranayama. Observation of this kind may be difficult if the attention is being pulled in other directions.

Pranayama can be mechanically practiced without full attention, but the fruit of the practice comes when attention is absorbed in the action. Full attention on the breath, in whatever method of pranayama employed, deeply internalizes awareness.

50. Pranayama modifies the breath internally, externally or in a suspended fashion. These modifications can be long and subtle and known through observation of location in the body, time of intervals and number.

51. The fourth modification of pranayama transcends internal or external experience.

52. Due to the fourth modification of pranayama, the veil that covers the light of consciousness is dispersed.

The state of a person's being can be discerned by observation of the breath. Forceful or erratic breathing can indicate distraction in the mind or a disturbance in the body. As awareness becomes internalized and peace prevails, the breath becomes subtler and more refined.

During episodes of deep meditation the breath may appear to cease all together. When this naturally occurs the inclination to surrender to higher samadhi states is near. Samadhi, being beyond what we can experience internally or externally, is possible during the fourth modification of practice.

By the practice of pranayama the yogi can move beyond the veils of ignorance that prevent the apprehension of the essence of reality. The mind and breath are linked. The mind can weave layers or conditioning that block out the truth of pure consciousness or it can be cleansed to reflect clearly the light of pure consciousness. Dedicated practice of the psycho-physiological techniques of pranayama restores the mind to its naturally reflective Sattvic state.

53. Pratyahara leads to perfect mastery of the senses.

The senses are the gates that carry our energy from our Self-realized soul nature to the world. Immersion in the world of experience directs energy away from our true Self. This leads to confusion that prevents the average person from understanding what they are at the core of their being, which eventually leads to suffering.

Pratyahara is the turning inward of our sensual energies. By stopping the flow of our attention to the world of experience and redirecting it inward to the source of our senses, attention is realigned with our eternal Self. Repeated practice of withdrawing the senses into the eternal Self during meditation enables one to live in the world while remaining connected to the source of the world, which is pure consciousness.

The senses are useful to function effectively through our mind and body. Pratyahara keeps the sense faculties healthy so we can perceive experiences clearly. Pratyahara also conserves our energy and prevents the depletion of life force, which can contribute to restlessness of the mind and also illness within the body.

The stages of yoga practice culminating in pratyahara are the external methods leading to oneness in the eternal Self. They are preparation for the internal disciplines that give birth to full liberation of consciousness in unqualified samadhi.

Chapter 7

QUALITIES OF SOUL UNFOLDMENT

Part 3: The Chapter on Powers of Accomplishment

1. *Dharana is the fixation of the field of being within a focal point.*

Dharana is the Sanskrit word for yogic concentration. Once we can effectively internalize our attention, the next step on the yogic path entails learning to concentrate. Concentration occurs when our awareness (individualized field of being) is internalized and we can, with practice, hold an object of contemplation steady in that awareness.

Concentration does not need to be stressful or tense. When practiced correctly, it is light, easy and refreshing. We are concentrating when we rest our attention on a flower in an autumn field, or when we are listening to the words of an interesting conversation. It happens naturally and effortlessly, and distractions are easily ignored.

Once our attention is internalized, we can focus it on a mantra, our concept of the divine, or simply the feeling of omnipresence.

2. *When a single thought directs the field of being to a chosen focal point, meditation (dhyana) occurs.*

With repeated practice, we can hold our awareness focused on a chosen object of contemplation for as long as we intend. When that focus is effortless, easy and consistent, we are meditating.

3. *The field of being reflects objects [focused on] alone, as if empty of its own essence, during Samadhi.*

Whatever we hold in our awareness, that is what we experience. If we hold the idea that we are a limited personality with a particular history and set of problems and preferences, that is what we will experience. Repeated focus on a particular idea, set of circumstances, or object will eventually precipitate the realization of that line of focus.

This is why it is recommended to adopt the view point that we are already enlightened while meditating. It begins the process of shifting our current experience to the enlightened ideal until we realize it as truth.

If we can wholeheartedly hold our attention on the ideal of Love, Divinity, Self-Knowledge, or Pure Consciousness, our field of being will reflect that reality as if that is all there is. Then we are practicing Samadhi with that ideal.

4. *The field of being is perfectly regulated by dharana, dhyana, and Samadhi practiced together as one.*

The practice of Yoga is meant to free us of our imagined limitations, that we may live happily and effectively in whatever realm we happen to inhabit and in whatever circumstances we find ourselves. Learning to regulate the field of being, through skillful concentration and mastery of attention, we can choose our experiences, moods and mindsets with greater ease. The mind, emotions and body more readily respond to our innate inclination toward peace and balance when the field of being is perfectly regulated through consistent practice of concentration, meditation and Samadhi.

5. *When these are practiced together, insight shines forth.*

Concentrated meditation to the stage of complete absorption into the object or ideal contemplated gives direct insight or knowledge into that object or ideal. Meditating on divine qualities until we are aware of nothing else, allows us to experience those divine qualities first hand. Then our insight is born of knowledge rather than belief. Knowledge from direct experience results from the combined skillful practice of concentration, meditation and Samadhi.

6. *The application is in stages.*

Beginning meditators are often unrealistic in their expectations of what meditation will be like for them. They often expect to have the same experience as meditators who have been practicing skillfully for years, multiple hours a day.

The first stage of meditation may involve learning to sit still and letting the thoughts and emotions settle. This is beneficial to the body and mind, allowing relaxation to occur. Depending on the individual and the amount of stress in the person's life, the time it takes to master this stage of practice can vary from days to months. Pranayama, or mantra practice are techniques to aid the process.

Once negative stress has been minimized and the meditator can quickly settle into a relaxed state during meditation, the next stage begins. Remaining alert and awake while relaxation occurs, the meditator now practices withdrawing attention from thoughts, emotions, memories, external sounds, feelings, etc.

This is like a turtle pulling its limbs into its shell. The meditator detaches attention from the changing external and internal phenomena of the world, and rests within. This is the practice of pratyahara, or sense withdrawal. This stage too, takes consistent practice to master.

In time, as attention can be held internally contemplating the chosen object or ideal, at the exclusion to all else, the meditator experiences complete absorption, and now develops the ability to maintain the state of Samadhi.

Unless we are natural born meditators, it can take years to master all of these stages. The only way we can naturally perform any endeavor is through consistent, attentive, interested practice. Otherwise, we are only going through the motions.

Just because an endeavor may be difficult, at first, is no reason to avoid practice until mastery is realized. Many people do not understand the value of complete yoga practice, because they give up when they experience difficulty at a particular stage of the process. Consistency and patience in practice, or even seeking out the counsel of someone who has already mastered the stage in question, can be of benefit.

We are all, at the core of our being, fully awake and realized. The difference between an accomplished yogi, and one who is not, is the degree of realization of this truth. Patient and attentive development of all the stages of yoga practice gives complete Self-realization. The time it takes for that to occur need not be an issue.

7. *The three inner limbs of yoga are distinct from the five outer limbs.*

The five outer limbs are yama (restraints), niyama (internal disciplines), asana (proper posture), pranayama (breath awareness and exercises), and pratyahara (internalization of attention) as described in the previous chapter.

The three inner limbs are dharana (concentration), dhyana (meditation), and Samadhi (realization of unified awareness). The inner limbs occur once attention is internalized.

8. *The inner limbs, however, are external to the seedless state of Samadhi.*

The seedless state of Samadhi occurs effortlessly. When Samadhi is as natural and easy as it is for a healthy person to breathe, it is seedless. It happens of its own accord. There is no need to do anything or undertake any practice for it to occur.

Since the inner limbs, although internalized, also take a degree of effort, they are considered external to the deeper realization of effortless Samadhi. Just as a musician learns to effortlessly play beautiful music through years of practice, so too can the practitioner of yoga learn to effortlessly exist in the seedless state of Samadhi. Then the soul is free, embodied or otherwise.

9. *When activity towards externalization is restricted and a tendency toward ending the fluctuations in the field of consciousness emerges, at that moment consciousness becomes clearer.*

The majority of the world's population, in this era, seeks external fulfillment. They look for the next person, event, or object to make them happy. This increases the fluctuations in the field of awareness, because for that external fulfillment to occur, there must always be something new, and something changing. Hence, fluctuations occur in the field of consciousness.

The moment we entertain the possibility that external changes may not lead to true fulfillment, it becomes easier to turn attention away from external seeking. As soon as we make the effort to turn our attention within, at that very moment, consciousness becomes clearer.

10. A calm flow of consciousness occurs due to its natural inclination.

When left alone, water remains smooth and calm. Similarly, when consciousness is internalized, or free of fluctuations caused by objectification, it is serene. This is its natural inclination.

Experiences, thoughts, feelings, and objects of perception have an inertia to them. They exist because we continue to give them attention. The more attention we give to an object of perception, the more power it has to remain in awareness. By gentle observation, without getting involved with or thinking about the perceptions within and around us, the force of inertia disperses. When the force is spent, the objects of awareness no longer prevent us from experiencing the natural tranquil state of consciousness.

11. All objectifying disappears transformed by one pointed absorption in the field of consciousness.

By engaging attention into one pointed contemplation, we are aware of nothing else. It is impossible to be aware of the sense of self and separateness while fully absorbed in the contemplation of Divinity, Love, or Pure Existence Being.

12. Then the contents of the field remain similar because of focused attention.

The field of being is then experienced only as that which is contemplated. This becomes easier to experience in meditation with each repeated successful session. Then, due to familiarity, it can also be experienced while not meditating.

13. *The elements and sense organs are transformed in regard to the characteristic form of consciousness, and the condition of consciousness.*

The sense organs are our abilities to hear, touch, taste, smell and see. The elements and their varied combinations are the basic aspects of nature that the sense organs perceive. The state of one's consciousness determines how the sense organs and the elements are transformed and experienced by the witnessing presence of our Self. The influential relationship between the Self, the state of consciousness, the sense organs and the elements provides the content for our life experiences.

14. *The characteristic form of the substrate (the deeper levels of consciousness) may be quieted, arisen or indistinguishable.*

Within each individualized unit of consciousness, there is the potential for numerous and varied experiences. This is why people's lives, even if presented with the same circumstances, can be so different from one another. The deeper levels of consciousness act as the store house for our potential physical, mental and emotional experiences.

When we are directly experiencing a mood, thought or situation, that potential is active, or arisen. When the experience is on the periphery of our awareness, not quite activated, it is considered quieted. If a potential experience exists deep within our consciousness, yet we are not yet aware of it, it is considered indistinguishable.

Yoga meditation aids the process of bringing awareness to all possibilities. This way we are not surprised by hidden or quieted subliminal triggers suddenly dominating our life experience. As Self-knowledge is revealed, we gain understanding of the potential strengths, weaknesses and triggers that are stored within the depths of our individualized consciousness.

As wisdom develops we can learn to avoid situations, thoughts or moods that have the potential to throw us into a state of unconsciousness. A state of unconsciousness can be likened to any experience where we become dominated by fears, phobias, compulsions or obsessions.

If we lose the ability to see or experience a situation with *inner* calm and clarity and respond inappropriately, it can be considered an unconscious state. If we can maintain our *inner* poise while being appropriate to the situation at hand it is an indication that our consciousness is free of influence from conditioning that, in the past, may have made us an automaton or slave to karma.

Conditioning that is quieted, or on the periphery of awareness can be neutralized through choice and strong intention in the present moment. Conditioning that is activated can be allowed to run its course with detached awareness, if it is not harmful. Otherwise it can be actively resisted and neutralized in the present by will and activities and thoughts that counter its influence. Conditioning that is indistinguishable and not presently in awareness can be silently dissolved through superconscious meditation practice.

> *15. The separateness of the sequential progression of each individualized field of consciousness is the reason for the separateness of transformations.*

In this infinite consciousness, this infinite universe, the possibilities of potential life experiences are also infinite. The sequence of expression of one's life experiences all depends on the order and arrangement of the inner conditioning. This is different for all individualized units of consciousness.

In Roy Eugene Davis' commentary on the Bhagavad Gita, entitled *The Eternal Way*, on page 194 he writes: "Because conditional mental states, degree of ability to comprehend, and the influences of the gunas on one's field of awareness, each soul's unfoldment experiences are unique. Therefore, it is stated that no other soul has ever experienced the manifestations of Consciousness exactly as this soul has perceived it."

Eventually, when we are no longer identified with any particular conditioning, the idea of a soul, or a sense of separateness, all life is experienced as one thing. This is why realized or enlightened people may say they see nothing but God and experience no sense of separateness. This is possible to be experienced in deep meditation, and eventually as normal, whether sitting in quiet meditation or being active in the world.

> 16. *Due to perfect dharana, dhyana, and samadhi practiced simultaneously on the characteristics, potential change, and condition of consciousness knowledge of the past and future is possible.*

This sutra begins the exploration of the "soul powers" that can result from consistent and effective spiritual practice.

By perfect concentration, sustained meditation, and full contemplative absorption on the characteristics, potential changes and the present condition of consciousness one can know the past and also the possible future.

Even without deep meditation, we can know the generalities of one's past and future. Consider that we are creatures of habit. Unless we are actively becoming more fully conscious, how we live, act, think and feel today is a good indication of how we will behave tomorrow. As long as we are alert and perceptive we can know the trends of the past and the future with a fair amount of accuracy.

> 17. *Confused understanding of words, meanings, and thoughts occur due to superimposition. By perfect regulation of consciousness, the meanings of sounds made by any being can be known.*

If we cannot understand another person's actions, words or ideas, it is because we are superimposing our own past experiences, ideas, and meanings on the situation. If we could perfectly detach our awareness from our personality and history and fully identify with another's history and personality, we would understand exactly why they do what they do, and say what they say.

The same is true for all creatures and beings. A bird, a mountain lion and a butterfly do not relate to the world in the same way as a human does. By regulating consciousness so that our own perceptions and understanding of life do not interfere, and listening to the noises, gestures and actions of another creature we understand what it is they want to communicate.

As with all the "soul powers" listed in this chapter, the first requirement for success is the ability to fully internalize attention, release attachment to the personality or the small sense of self, and be able to concentrate, meditate, and experience full absorption in that which is contemplated. If this is not possible, results will be mixed, if at all successful, and may result in false imagination.

False imagination is more common among people who openly talk about these experiences. The "soul powers" are not for entertainment or conversation, they are meant only to assist the awakening soul along its path of evolution and maturation into full Self-realization.

18. By direct perception of subliminal triggers, knowledge of previous incarnations is acquired.

During meditation, subconscious conditioning may rise into awareness as a random thought, mood, vision or memory. These can be caused by recent experiences or experiences in the distant past which have not yet been processed or digested.

We can exhaust the subliminal triggers by allowing them to rise and fall as a detached observer. The moment we are pulled into these triggers and identify with them, their influence on our consciousness is sustained. Taking a deep breath and reestablishing our selves as the witnessing presence breaks the identification. In time, the images, feelings or memories lose their force and dissolve. Then we are free of their influence. All that remains is our pure conscious nature.

19. By direct perception of the arising thoughts, an-other's state of consciousness can be known.

In a mentally quiet and neutral state we can attune to another person by intention. Thoughts or sensations may be perceived giving an indication of the other person's current state of consciousness. This can be helpful when determining how supportive a relationship may be for us. If the state of consciousness is confused or disturbed, we can avoid it. If it is light, clear and Self-shining, it can be a supportive relationship.

It is often recommended to attune to one's guru or teacher for this reason. By intending to know the state of con-sciousness of the guru, we can temporarily understand what the guru understands, and experience what the guru experiences. Of course, this is only helpful if the guru is clear and healthy-minded.

During group meditations, if the leader is a proficient meditator, we can benefit by tuning into the leader. We will learn through osmosis how to better meditate and get a temporary boost to our efforts.

20. Knowing the state of another person's awareness does not support that state, because the intention is to gain insight rather than identify with what is known. Identification remains as consciousness alone.

When gaining insight into another person's awareness as described in sutra 19, we keep our awareness identified as infinite formless consciousness, while observing the other's state of consciousness with detached interest. In this way, we do not support nor do we get caught up in the other's state of consciousness. We are only gathering information. Confusion can result if we lose our objectivity, which we want to avoid.

If it is necessary to practice this "soul power", imagine that you are looking at a slide under a microscope. The scientist studying organisms under a microscope does not have to come into contact or be influenced by that which is studied. The scientist only has to observe and make notes free of judgment. Then the necessary information is gathered. The same detached observation is practiced to effectively know another's state of consciousness.

> 21. *Sanyama on the form of the body with the intention to prevent light from being deflected, one becomes invisible because of interiorization of attention.*

We can avoid detection by not drawing attention to our self. By withdrawing our thought field into the body, we can exist or move as if invisible. This is why someone in deep meditation, with attention turned completely within can often go unnoticed.

> 22. *Karma is either fast or slow in fruition. Knowledge of the time of death may be known by perfect contemplation on the speed of karmic fruition, or by signs.*

By contemplating the characteristics and timing of one's life path, the end of events and even one's death can be known.

The universe is one whole reality. Everything is related to everything else. With practice, we can know the outcome of an event by observing the signs and quality of other events happening simultaneously.

> 23. *Perfect contemplation on friendliness gives spiritual strength.*

A person lacking friendliness is at odds with him or her self. It shows a deep seated feeling of separation and isolation. By contemplation and extension of feelings of friendliness, the sense of separation and isolation are neutralized and the experience of life as a whole, seamless, supportive reality is known. This gives spiritual strength as our practice becomes empowered with compassion and understanding.

Friendliness need not cause us hardship or give others the right to take advantage of us. We can be friendly and compassionate to people with ill intentions, without being subjected to those intentions. If we know the person we are interacting with is a thief or a liar, we can maintain a sense of compassionate goodwill, without losing sight of their potential influence on our life. Then we can interact with the person appropriately.

> 24. *Perfect contemplation on the strength of an elephant gives physical strength.*

Contemplation of physical strength, seeing the body healthy and strong, directs us to make choices that bring about that reality. The body can also be subtly influenced by our perceptions, thoughts and ideas. Holding a vision of strength while taking intelligent action to develop that strength will give results according to the intention.

25. *By projection of the finer light of consciousness, knowledge of that which is subtle, concealed or distant can be known.*

In deep meditation, the light of consciousness can be seen in our mind's eye, and even experienced as the fullness of our being. When that light is experienced, we can intend to pierce that light or expand beyond it and move completely beyond body consciousness.

As body consciousness is released we are free of the limiting characteristics of time and location. Then, through gentle intention, we can know what is subtle, concealed, or distant, because we are not bound by any obstacle of personality, time or space.

26. *Perfect contemplation on the sun, reveals knowledge of the planes of existence.*

By contemplation on the inner light, direct knowledge about the processes of creation and the finer levels of existence dawns. The knowledge need not be revealed as words or data. The knowledge is an internal knowing and direct imparting of what is true. Through this knowledge we gain insight into the fullness of our being, from pure consciousness, to the subtle mental and energetic fields, to the densest material creation.

If the inner light is not easily seen in meditation, it can help to imagine a radiant sun in the mind's eye and let that be the focus of contemplation until awareness is fully absorbed in the experience. In time the imagination will give way to the actual experience of the inner sun.

Being able to stay alert, yet relaxed as the light is revealed is key. The moment tension or anxious expectation arises the inner light will vanish. It can be exciting when we first see the inner light, as it is brilliant and qualitatively different from our imagination or brain produced phenomena. That excitement almost always effectively neutralizes the experience. Relax, invite and let it happen.

Seeing the inner light needs to be treated as though it is the most natural experience in the world.

27. On the moon, gives knowledge of the stars.

The moon represents our memories, past and the reflected light of pure consciousness as the ego-personality. The stars represent our karmic state. This is why astrology is utilized to understand our potential life path. Through the study of the stars we can understand the ego-personality's karmic potential. Each of the planets, which look like stars from earth, reflects a particular life experience, or karma.

By contemplating the disc of the moon, or visualizing it in our mind's eye, knowledge of our karmic potential, or the stars, can be known.

28. On the pole star, gives knowledge of the stars motion.

The pole star is virtually a fixed star in the night's sky. All other celestial objects are seen to rotate around it. By contemplating that fixed star, knowledge of the motions of heavenly bodies is acquired.

The pole star also represents our inner consciousness which is changeless and timeless. By contemplating and identifying with that changeless and timeless aspect of our being, the changing and temporal aspects are understood properly.

29. On the navel chakra, gives knowledge of the bodies internal states.

By holding attention, with expectation of discovery, at the navel of the body, the current state of the physical body can be known.

30. On the well in the throat, brings cessation of hunger and thirst.

With repeated practice, holding attention at the throat chakra can neutralize physical hunger and thirst. It can also neutralize addictive cravings and compulsive desires.

31. On the manubrium, give steadiness.

The manubrium is the bone at the center of the rib cage at the front of the torso. This is related to the heart chakra. When awareness is maintained effortlessly at the heart chakra, our states of consciousness becomes steady. We are less inclined to be influenced by external experiences of phenomena.

32. On the light in the crown chakra, gives visions of perfected beings.

The crown chakra at the top of the skull is an excellent point for contemplation. It has been said, that if we could simply hold our attention at the crown for a long enough duration, we would naturally move into permanent enlightened realization.

The crown chakra is not associated with any limited state. It is boundless and infinite in experience. When we are able to hold attention at the crown, existing as an infinite boundless being, we can experience visions of other perfected beings. What is most important is experiencing the vision of our Self as a perfected being.

33. *In a flash of illumination, all knowledge is provided.*

Knowledge, as referred to in the Yoga Sutras, is not data or a collection of concepts and ideas, it is direct experience of what is true. It occurs in a flash.

As the mind becomes quiet, there is spaciousness within our individualized consciousness. In that spaciousness we can be curious about what it is we want to know. What is it like to be only pure consciousness, with no limitations or conditioning? What is my relationship with the wholeness of life? What is God? What is Om? What am I? If we are sincerely curious about these matters, and we sustain this curiosity in the quiet of focused meditation, flashes of insight about the chosen topic will happen.

Think of this process like a conversation. If we are interested in getting information through questioning, we first ask our question, then we wait for the response. We only have to ask the question once with intention, and then remain alert and watchful for the response. We do not repeat the question over and over like a mantra or other technique. Having already practiced our meditation techniques, we are established in the alert yet tranquil state of meditation. Repeating the question over and over, is like trying to get an answer from a friend, but never giving the friend time to respond. We must wait quietly for the answer.

Of course, this does not work like any normal conversation between people, and so the time between asking the question with expectant curiosity and the waiting may be a short or a long time. We may even need to repeat the process throughout multiple meditation sessions. However long it takes, that is how long we continue our inquiry. The answer always comes in a flash of insight and then it is as if we had the knowledge all along.

34. Perfect contemplation on the heart reveals full knowledge of the field of consciousness.

At first, holding attention in the physical heart center will bring peace and stability to the field of being. From this peaceful stable place, we are free to turn attention further within, withdrawing attention completely from body consciousness.

Then we contemplate the heart of our being. This is the very essence and support for all our experiences. It is our eternal nature beyond time and space. It is that Seer that existed when we were dreaming last night, when we were playing in the park at the age of four, when we were working on our report for work two weeks ago, and will persist through each and every experience. It was before birth, and will be after death. It is beyond our personality, our sense of self. It is beyond our history and our preferences.

What is That, which exists through out all changing phenomena? That is the heart that reveals full knowledge of the field of consciousness. Know That, and know everything.

> 35. *Experience does not distinguish between the constituents of matter and the Self. By perfect contemplation on what exists of itself as distinct from that which exists for experience, knowledge of the Self is revealed.*

Experience is anything that can be perceived. Dreams, thoughts, feelings are all in the realm of experience. Pain, people, pleasure, states of consciousness are all things. They exist simply that we may have experiences. That which experiences all these phenomena can be considered distinct from the phenomena, because no matter what experiences rise or fall, the experiencer remains.

By discernment we distinguish the difference between the permanent and the impermanent. At first this may be an intellectual or intuitive understanding. This is not full knowledge. When total knowledge of the Self dawns, there will be no question about its reality. It will not require intuition or intellectual reasoning or remembrance. It will be as evident and obvious as the sun shining overhead on a cloudless day.

Then we understand why the skillful yogis say that there is nothing to fear in the world, and that pleasure, pain, obsession and compulsion are based on inaccurate knowledge of what is true. We will understand that there is nothing but the Self, the eternal changeless reality. We will know the freedom of Self-realization and it will not be an idea or a belief to be hoped for, but a simple and obvious fact of existence.

36. *From that flash of illumination superior powers of the senses of hearing, feeling, seeing, tasting, smelling and intelligence occur.*

With each flash of illumination consciousness becomes clearer, and less fragmented. Conscious awareness expands beyond the confines of normal human perception. We then can know and perceive things that are not commonly known through the limited senses. This is only because our awareness of our self is expanding beyond a limited individualized state, and is growing into the fullness of our actual omnipresent and omniscient being. It is not special, it is the maturation of the field of being, that can occur when the obstacles to that maturation are removed.

When this power dawns, it is not experienced as something fantastic. Often it happens as naturally as breathing. There is no premeditation.

We happen to say something that was perfectly appropriate to the person next to us. It answered a question that they were pondering without even verbalizing it to us. We delay our travels by a half hour without thinking about it, only to find that had we left earlier we may have missed an important phone call or opportunity.

The clarity and expansiveness of our consciousness is aware of itself to a greater degree, and so knows these things without the aid of the mind or personality.

37. These soul powers, when externalized are obstacles to the seedless state of Samadhi.

As mentioned previously, if we actively try to cultivate these powers so that we may display pride in their accomplishment we will not achieve the seedless state of Samadhi. By externalizing and drawing attention to these powers for others to see, we are only strengthening the ego, the false sense of self. This confines our awareness, which is counter to the process of Self-realization.

If these powers arise naturally, without premeditation, as they often do at the appropriate time, they are acceptable. Otherwise our focus is on clarity, expansion and realizing the eternal nature of our essence of being.

If we have experienced and mastered any of these powers, and need to utilize them to assist in our internal conscious evolution, that is acceptable. For example, if we are experiencing a difficult life situation and need to maintain our stability and poise as the experience exhausts itself, it is appropriate to refer to sutra 31 of this chapter, *"On the manubrium, give steadiness"*. If we are experiencing a physical difficulty it may be appropriate to meditate on sutra 29 of this chapter, *"On the navel chakra, gives knowledge of the bodies internal states."* Also, the sutras related to further clarifying awareness and realizing the fullness of our being, will help the natural unfoldment of Samadhi.

38. By relaxing attachment to relationship to the body, and projecting consciousness forth, another's body can be entered.

It is only the tenacious identification that we are bound to a specific body that prevents us from knowing another body. When that identification is released, consciousness is free to change points of view as it will.

> *39. Mastering the upward flowing life force enables one to rise above harmful conditions in nature.*

Consciousness is fully supportive of realizing its eternal nature. By directing our attention and life force up through the spine, into the higher chakras and brain centers, we lift our awareness out of involvement with subconscious conditioning and confusion.

Metaphorically, the "wholeness of our consciousness" takes note of this intention. Seeing the individualized aspect of itself making an effort to rise out of the mire of limited ignorance, it removes many of the harmful conditions that otherwise create hardship in the life experience. Then the process of Self-realization becomes easier.

Also, by keeping our attention in the higher chakras we are less driven by compulsions, fears, desires and obsessions, and so make better choices. This also leads to avoidance of distracting, pain-producing experience.

> *40. Physical radiance occurs by mastering the nourishing life force in the navel that regulates bodily functions.*

In sutra 29 of this chapter, we learned that meditation on the navel center gives knowledge of the bodies internal states. With this knowledge we can change our behavior to make the body healthier.

The life force at the navel is said to distribute the nourishment from our food to the body. By meditating on the navel, we also increase our digestive fire, so that our digestion is improved, thereby aiding the availability of nourishment to our cells and tissues. A well nourished body is radiant, with a healthy glow.

The life force at the navel can also be stimulated through various breathing techniques which involve particular muscular contraction of the abdomen and pelvic floor. These can be learned from a yoga teacher educated in such processes.

> *41. Subtle divine sounds can be heard by contemplating the relationship between hearing and the ethers.*

By giving attention to the ears, and the subtle sounds within the ears and around the head, a frequency or tone can often be heard underneath the usual sounds of our environment. This is easier to hear in very quiet places, or in holy places, where deep prayer or meditation has occurred on a consistent basis.

Once we hear that first consistent frequency, all of our attention is directed to it. We listen more intently and deeper. We listen to any constant sounds underneath of the original sound. This takes practice and a high level of concentration. It can help to hold attention at the spiritual eye center in the forehead, or at the crown at the top of the skull.

When we can hold our awareness on these subtle sounds, while listening more intently, eventually we will be aware of nothing else but full absorption in sound. Eventually the sounds may merge and the roar of an ocean fills awareness. This occurs just before total Samadhi.

42. Contemplation of the body in relation to etheric space results in lightness of the body.

By being simultaneously aware of the body, while imagining and feeling as though the body extends through space, throughout the universe, a sense of lightness and ease will arise. Once again, maintaining attention at the crown chakra during practice aids this process.

43. Contemplation on states beyond the physical realm results in dispersing of the coverings that sheath the Self.

In order to have an experience in this world, and in this particular time-line we need a vehicle to relate to the time-space continuum. This vehicle is made up of various coverings. The physical body is considered the gross or material sheath. We also have an energetic sheath, which is the accumulation of our consistent emotional states. The causal sheath, is the body of thought and concepts. All of these sheaths together create the vehicle which gives rise to our individualized experiences in consciousness, our particular life situation and circumstance.

In order to experience states beyond the physical realm, we have to drop or let go of our accustomed attachment to the physical, energetic and causal bodies. Then we are free to experience what we choose at will. This can be likened to going on vacation. In order to arrive at the beach, you must first let go of your attachment to home, and remove your self from home. Otherwise, it is impossible to physically arrive at the beach.

As maturing units of individualized consciousness we are all learning to disperse and release attachment to the coverings of the Self. Once the coverings are dispersed, only the Self remains. When we realize it is safe and acceptable to exist solely as the Self, free of identification of limiting factors, we are free.

> 44. *Contemplation on the gross states, the essential nature, the subtle states and the purpose of matter results in mastery of the elements.*

Through deep contemplation on the relationship and purpose of the gross and subtle states of consciousness mastery of the elements is possible.

Once we know the mechanics of any system we can become masters of that system. Through the process of Self discovery we learn the mechanics of existence, from understanding the tiniest atom, to the basic behaviors of living a constructive life, to the profoundest states of consciousness.

Consistent and attentive contemplation and study on how anything works, eventually results in knowledge and mastery.

> 45. *From the knowledge acquired one may become minute, perfect in body, and non afflicted by the bodies constitution.*

Knowledge allows us to act in order to achieve what we desire.

46. Perfection of the body results in grace, strength, and adamantine firmness.

Living in harmony with the laws of nature gives strength, grace and the ability to avoid, endure and resist physical adversity.

47. By contemplating the processes of perception, one's essential nature, the sense of individualized "I am", and the interconnectedness of the purpose of the senses, one gains mastery over the sense organs.

We are led to compulsive behavior to gratify the senses only when we think that gratification of the senses will lead to happiness. As we are all seeking happiness in one way or another, all activity is based on that primal drive.

When there is confusion about our true nature, we seek happiness in objects or situations that are impermanent and so eventually lead to sorrow. Anything that can come into our life will eventually disappear. To seek out happiness through transient phenomena surely invites sorrow, eventually.

By contemplating how life experience continuously changes in our perception, we make peace with the impermanence of the world and its things. No longer do we foolishly expect that which always changes, to act contrary to its nature.

As we contemplate our own essential nature as the changeless witnessing presence behind, supporting, and experiencing the world of perception we remember the one eternal reality. This is our very Self.

Still a sense of individualized awareness may remain. In time, as contemplation continues, that too will dissolve. Left with what is, and what has always been, the purpose of the world of sensation and the sense organs is realized.

Then we are naturally the master of our senses and sense organs. Sensory stimulation is no longer necessary to remain tranquil and fulfilled. Those people, places and activities that we thought would provide fulfillment no longer exert an influence over us. Now we are free to choose our activities and experiences without compulsion, and without the false idea that we will find true fulfillment in any experience.

This is as natural as a child growing into adulthood. The things that we enjoyed as a child or teenager, do not call to us. The rattle or toy, which seemed so important for our happiness when we were babies holds no interest. The intoxicants, adrenaline or drama we enjoyed as an adolescent have no power. Even the most refined tastes or desires of a normal mature adult will be resolved into Self-knowledge.

> 48. *From that contemplation one gains swiftness of mind, transcendence of the sense organs and master of the primary matrix of matter.*

Then anything is possible as consciousness.

Deep realization of this truth is necessary for this sutra to be actualized. The extremely rare sages and masters who have that degree of mastery did not develop that mastery by only meditating once a day and half-heartedly trying to realize their Self.

Consider a master of any normal art or enterprise. Those rare individuals worked tirelessly, studied, practiced and committed more hours a day than most people are awake for years on end to attain their aim. This gives us an idea of what is required for yoga mastery.

Now we need not be discouraged by this. It does not mean that we need to lock ourselves away in a cave for years and lifetimes. It only means that we need to have a regular meditation and contemplation practice that we are enthused about. At other times we give our full commitment to living the principles outlined in this text. Then every moment of every day incrementally leads to remembrance of our transcendent identity.

> 49. *Identified only with the separateness of sattva guna and the Self, one gains omniscience and supremacy over all states.*

Sattva guna is the complete and total experience and state of light, joy, bliss, and fulfillment. Identified only with sattva guna and the eternal witnessing presence we exist as the all, manifest and unmanifest, and have supremacy over all states. No longer are we subject to the changing states of consciousness. They are subject only to the Self.

> 50. *Through non attachment to even this pure omniscient state, the impediments to the all oneness of seeing the seer vanish.*

Even the attachment to sattva guna, and the pure omniscience of the Self will eventually be transcended for our freedom to be complete. Once free of that attachment, that which is seen, the act of seeing, and the seer itself vanish.

This is beyond words, concepts and description. We can imagine what it would be like and try to describe it, but only direct experience will suffice.

> 51. *Upon awakening to this high state, pride of accomplishment will cause a reversion to former conditioned inclinations.*

If there are any subtle attachments or subconscious unresolved concepts or notions left, the false sense of self can give rise to spiritual pride. Should this be allowed to take root and grow, we can revert to former states of consciousness.

In reality, we cannot fully awaken to this higher state unless there is absolutely nothing left to generate pride or sense of accomplishment. If the possibility of reversion to former conditions exists, it means we have not fully completed the process, and are still deluding our self in some way.

> 52. *By contemplation on the present moment and its sequential progression, discernment between sattva guna and the Self is born.*

Sattva guna, even though it is one of the purest experiences this side of full Self-realization, is still a support for changing phenomena. This gives rise to a sense of time.

Contemplating the experience of light, joy, bliss and fulfillment as they are sustained through time, leads to the realization that the Self is even untouched and not influenced by such pleasant states.

The common belief is that Self-realization results in constant bliss and happiness. Bliss and happiness are also defining characteristics and are impermanent. We can make choices that sustain the experience of bliss and happiness, but this should not be mistaken for Self-realization.

In the beginning practices of yoga, we are often impelled to release attachment to negative or painful states. This is commonly advised and the smart thing to do. When we are happier it makes it easier for us to undertake more challenging tasks, such as exploring complete and total soul liberation.

Many people realize freedom from negative states and then do not proceed to release attachment to positive states as well. For Self-realization to be complete, attachment to any state of consciousness needs to be released.

53. *From that, ascertaining the difference between similar events, which cannot otherwise be distinguished, is possible due to lack of categorical, potential and positional restrictions.*

Once we can discern the difference between sattva guna and the Self, we are supremely free and unbound by restricting influences. Restricting influences include our tendency to categorize information and the assessment of potential events based on past experiences. Positional restrictions refer to our position in consciousnesses or our point of view. This can include identification with a personality, history, body, race, or any state where we are identified with anything other than the eternal Self.

Any point of view is a restricting influence. If we are identified with a point of view, we will experience any phenomena through that point of view and our information will not be completely objective or unbiased. When we are free of restricting influences we can distinguish the truth of things clearly.

Events often occur which seem similar and seem to have similar causes even when there is no similar cause. When we are not attributing an incorrect cause to an event, it is easier to understand the true cause of what is occurring.

> 54. *This knowledge, born of discernment, crosses beyond and encompasses all objective, temporal and non-sequential perceptions.*

Self-knowledge which arises from accurate discernment is above and beyond all experiential perceptions. Because of this, the knowledge of the Self results in wisdom which allows us to understand and interact with the world appropriately, free of delusion, illusion, compulsions, aversions and obsessions.

Once Self-knowledge dawns, in the words of the sage Vasistha, we are able to "live a natural and spontaneous life, contentedly."

> 55. *When the purity of sattva and the Self are equal, there is only Self-realization.*

When our internal experience is a perfect balance of complete Self-identification and sattvic living, there is only Self-realization.

Chapter 8

FINAL LIBERATION

Part 4: The Chapter on the Aloneness of Seeing

> 1. *Exceptional powers result from Samadhi, from in-fluences at birth, herbs, mantra, and intensity in spiritual practice.*

The spiritual growth process is less about achieving an end result, and more about growing into the fullness of our Infinite Self. Exceptional soul powers can result from Samadhi that is direct realization of our unity as the One Reality, manifest and unmanifest, timeless and finite. When we are aware of our full potential and understand the mechanics of reality, we can do, know and be things that seem miraculous.

When we are infants we are at the mercy of our surroundings and the people around us. As we grow up, we learn skills which enable us to live freely. We can buy a home, travel the world, explore various vocations, careers and hobbies, interact with people of our choosing. To the child, this is a mystery and a wonder, and something often longed for. When we are spiritual children we are subject to our helpful elders and guides. As we grow up, into healthy, responsible, well adjusted spiritual adults, we are no longer bound by the laws of childhood.

From an astrological viewpoint, the potential that we bring with us into this life is the result of our consistent past actions, tendencies, habits and choices. We are then born at the precise moment that reflects those astrological patterns.

If we have developed a musical skill consistently over lifetimes, it will be easier for us to develop that skill in this lifetime. Any skill or aspect of life that arises effortlessly in our experience is the result of past activity continuing into the present. This is also true of soul powers.

One may have all the resources that they need in this life and be wealthy because they are spiritually awake, and those resources are necessary for one's purpose in this incarnation. One may have all the resources they need because they spent many lifetimes understanding how to acquire wealth, and so that experience continues. Because soul powers are skills that can be developed through practice they are not indications of wisdom or spiritual understanding.

Plant substances can, in the right environment, and with the correct guidance provide glimpses of what naturally results from Samadhi. However, the effects of herbs are temporary and are rarely utilized effectively in the current era. One needs to be psychologically healthy and in the presence of a guide who is also responsible, experienced and psychologically healthy.

Mantras are words or word phrases that are said to be imbued with power. The meaning of the mantra indicates the power that can be developed from it. For example, "Om Namaha Shivaya" is a mantra that means, "I acknowledge with reverence the one Infinite Consciousness." Attuning to this power, and practicing this mantra can result in realization of the one Infinite Consciousness. Mantras need to be practiced with attention, enthusiasm, receptivity and over a long period of time for their results to occur.

Intensity in spiritual practice results in Samadhi. As mentioned at the beginning of this chapter, Samadhi naturally develops soul powers appropriate to the current life situation.

2. *The transformation into another category of existence is due to the overflowing of the primary unmanifest (ground of being).*

There is One Reality. It is self referring and self aware. It is infinite. There is no end to it, neither in time nor in space. There is no moment when it does not exist. We are that One Reality, and so the same is true for us. (Remember, because we need words to communicate, we have to use terms like "One Reality", "Us", "You", "I". They all refer to aspects of the same thing.)

Once our identification with a particular form is outgrown, a transformation of our identity seems to occur. This can happen as a physical death, or a change of any circumstance. The One Reality remains ever what it was, but its identification shifts.

Let us imagine a flower growing. At first there is the seed in the earth. The earth and the seed are like the unmanifest ground of being. Then it begins to grow. A green sprout emerges. The seed, which was one category of existence, outgrew its form in time and space. It then overflowed into the sprout, which is another category of existence. The sprout now continues the overflowing, and becomes a young plant with leaves. That overflowing continues until the category of existence is finally transformed into a flower. Then the transformation of decay begins and the process continues.

Being a human is one category of existence that resulted from many transformations of the One Reality. Human life itself has countless transformations. That life continues always overflowing into a new category. Even after being a human, there will be infinite transformations. This is one reason why non-attachment is so important. If we remain attached to or stuck at a particular stage of transformation, we will cause harm to ourselves by not letting the ground of being to continue its process.

3. *Samadhi does not motivate the process of (spiritual) evolution. It merely separates the obstacles (to its realization), like a farmer irrigates a field by removing obstacles to the flow of water.*

Consistent Samadhi practice removes the obstacles to knowing and being fully Self-realized. The light of Self-realization is as free and plentiful and omnipresent as the light of the Sun. It is always shining forth. Being identified with a limited small sense of self, is like wearing a blindfold, or staying behind closed doors. With each immersion in Samadhi, we get closer to untying the blindfold, or opening the doors and the windows to let the light in. Spiritual practice does not make anything happen, it removes the obstacles to knowing what has always been true.

This is why consistent spiritual practice is so important, and why we continue until the job is done. Once the ditches have been dug to irrigate the field, the water flows freely. Once our immersion in Samadhi is continuous, it continues of its own accord. Then all we have to do is make sure the irrigation pathways stay clear so the garden continues to grow. Then we meditate and continue on our spiritual path (living our infinite life) because it is a joy to do so.

4. *Individualized fields of being are brought into existence only from the sense separation, or notion "I am".*

The moment there is a sense of being separate, or a notion that "I am", an individualized field develops. This is the root of all ignorance, that there is an "I am" separate from everything else. There is only the One Reality. When there is no question that all is the One Reality and it is experienced beyond words, the individualized field merges back into the infinite.

Realized teachers have encouraged their students to inquire into the reality of the sense of "I am". They are encouraged to contemplate it until they know exactly what it really is. At the end of the inquiry, they realize it was a concept with no corresponding reality. Concepts do enable us to have experiences in time and space. They are as true and real as characters in a story book that exist only for the sake of the story.

5. *Although there is the sense of diverse activity, all individualized fields of being are motivated by the one un-individualized field.*

At night when dreaming, there are many diverse characters, places, and objects within the dream. They all exist as manifestations of the dreamer's psyche. They are not different from the dreamer. Similarly, all the diverse activities, points of view, and individualized fields of being are motivated and exist in and as the one infinite reality.

6. *Of the various activities, meditation results in non-accumulation of karma.*

Karma accumulates when we are invested in and attached to the results of our actions. Attachment is like glue. It causes our ideas and concepts to stick to our awareness. Every action motivated by a compulsive need or desire to accomplish something, is one more attachment creating activity that builds up identification with a personality, our false sense of self.

Think of a goal you once had, how you identified with it so strongly, that it was all you could think about. Obstacles that arose to prevent that goal created even more passion to achieve and accomplish the desired end. As attachment and desire increased, so did your identification with a personality that needed to achieve something. When the goal was realized, your false sense of self grew stronger. "I achieved that!" If you utterly failed in your attempt, the false sense of self also grew stronger. "I failed miserably." Through identifying with the varied actions of life, you build up the false sense of self and perpetuate the delusion of being a limited human being.

Meditation properly practiced withdraws attention from identification with external phenomena. It creates space, so that we can step back and watch the wheel of life rotating. With this distance, we no longer add momentum to identifying with thoughts, actions, objects, etc.

Beginning meditators often feel that they are practicing improperly because their mind is still filled with thoughts, ideas, concepts, memories, etc. If beginning meditators can allow the thoughts, etc. to pass, remaining as a detached observer, then they are practicing effectively. In the beginning, watching thoughts pass, being aware of memories, or witnessing the fact that we feel like a separate entity from the universe, are all acceptable so long as we do not get pulled into identifying with those things. By remaining as the alert witnessing presence of all that arises within awareness eventually those changes and fluctuations will lose their momentum, and all that remains is the Self. Because of this, meditation does not lead to the accumulation of karma.

Also, remember that while practicing your daily meditation it is good to avoid feeling that you are doing something special. Otherwise, your meditation practice is then accumulating karma, as you are building up a sense of self by defining your self as a meditator.

Think of meditation as though it is as natural as breathing. We don't walk around claiming we are breathers. Nor do we need to walk around dramatizing or proclaiming our spiritual practice. Keeping this in mind will prevent your spiritual path from turning into another karma-creating personality-centered activity.

7. *The karma of a one who is ending the fluctuations in the field of being, is neither good nor bad. Of others, it is threefold.*

Remember that yoga practice is the ending of the fluctuations in the field of consciousness. One who is practicing yoga meditation is acting to this end. This activity is neither good or bad, because it is not concerned with duality. The activity of others contributes to either beneficial constructive results, negative destructive results, or neutral benign results.

8. *The threefold karma of others results in the manifestation and corresponding fruition of subliminal traits.*

The constructive, neutral, or destructive actions of others gives an outlet for the subliminal tendencies that are within the mind and consciousness.

9. *Experiences that result from subliminal activators may seem like other experiences even when separated by birth, location and time. They are related by memory and similarity of subconscious causes.*

The human drama is fairly consistent in its themes of experience. Look to the genres of literature, from horror to comedy to romance to tragedy, and you will see in those genres the common experiences of the human condition. These experiences persist, life after life, year after year, and day after day. This repetition continues so long as there are subliminal activators.

If we are children and experience violence towards us, this is because of a subliminal activator in our consciousness. Good fortune and happiness as a child is also the result of subliminal activators. Subliminal activators are like receptor sites for a particular experience. We have the receptor site, and when we are in a situation where that receptor site can be activated, we experience that particular event.

Now in adulthood, if we still have that subliminal activators for violence or good fortune, we have the potential to experience events similar to our childhood years, except in the context of adulthood.

Life experiences do not change in a qualitative way until we come to terms with or neutralized our subliminal activators. Otherwise similar experiences, whether good or bad, will continue to arise in our life situation as the environment permits. Kriya Yoga neutralizes subliminal activators.

10. The will to live is eternal. The subliminal causes for life experience is beginningless.

Spirit and nature are eternal. They can be considered two sides of the same coin. We can imagine spirit to be that infinite witnessing presence in which all things occur. We can imagine nature to be the changing (yet eternal) material creation.

The continuous process of spirit becoming fascinated and involved with nature is eternal. If spirit (our Self or witnessing presence) wants to become involved in nature, it can find an infinite variety of reasons, because there is an infinite, beginningless and endless pool of subliminal causes, to do so.

Yoga practice is often treated as therapy. Therapy looks for reasons (subliminal activators) for why things are the way they are, and why negative experiences occur. Therapy can be useful to help us over come severe mental aberrations and to help us live an organized, productive life, but it cannot help us realize the root cause of unhappiness and ignorance. That is the realm of yoga as taught by Self-realized sages and undertaken by sincere practitioners.

This sutra clearly states that subliminal causes for life experiences are beginningless, also implying that they are endless and eternal. If we are looking for reasons why certain things happen, we have an infinite number of choices from which to draw.

If in meditation a thought or emotion arises, it is not something to be contemplated. We don't ask, "what does that mean?" or "why did I have that negative feeling?" Doing this draws us into involvement with that subliminal activator, and thereby sustains it. If such an experience occurs, we simply return our attention to our meditation technique disregarding the distraction. In time, our attachment to those thoughts or feelings will dissolve since we consistently will not feed them with our attention.

We can find a reason for anything, and the more we look for reasons the more we will find. With this knowledge we can cease looking for reasons, and do what is necessary. That is to detach from or rise above identification with karma. That is done by practicing the methods outlined in this work.

11. The absence of Self-awareness, the results of karma and supporting objects of experience [karma] are all interconnected. Upon the disappearance of these factors, [karmic] conditioning also disappears.

Absence of Self-awareness is the prime cause for involvement in karma. When there is absence of Self-awareness, there is involvement with karma and the objects which support karma. When absence of Self-awareness ends, the conditioning factors of karma also end. Similarly, by intentional detached meditation, and by withdrawing attention from the supporting objects of experience, Self-awareness naturally arises. When there is nothing left to perceive, only the Self remains.

This is why we practice training our awareness to withdraw from identification with the state of the body, the thoughts in the mind, the emotions, our history, or any other aspect of our lives that typically defines us. By closing our eyes and turning inwards, letting go of these attachments, we naturally become more Self aware.

12. Past and future exist owing to the sequential progression (difference) of characterized (perceived) forms.

To experience timelessness we need to withdraw our attention from the changing experiences of life. Anything that can be perceived, changes. We are aware of time because we see changes occurring in the forms around us. By disengaging from perception of forms, we disengage from time.

> *13. These forms are manifested or subtle and are composed of the primary forces of nature.*

Forms can be as obvious as the chair on which we sit, or they can be as subtle as a distant memory of which we are only dimly aware. Subtle or obvious, all forms are composed of combinations of the primary forces of nature: Sattva, Rajas, and Tamas.

> *14. The reality of an object is due to the uniqueness of its transformations.*

Objects appear because of uniqueness, which is a form of separateness. If there was no sense of separateness, there would be no object.

The reality of our personalities are the same. They exist because of a sense of separateness. There cannot be a personality unless there is a uniqueness and a feeling of separation from the environment.

> *15. Objects of perception are perceived differently due to the difference in [individualized] fields of being.*

How we perceive our environment is based solely on the particular conditioning of our particular view point. This difference in conditioning is what makes person A perceive a situation differently than person B. Where person

A sees an overwhelming challenge, person B sees a unique opportunity for growth.

> *16. An objects existence is not dependant on the perception of any particular [individualized] field of being.*

Objects exist whether they are perceived or not. To say that something does not exist because you are not there to experience it, is due to confusion. Objects persist so long as there is a universe in manifestation.

> *17. Objects are perceived if they are within the conditioning of the perceiving field of being.*

The world is filled with various objects, people and circumstances. Yet, we are only aware of those objects, people and circumstances with which we share a common inner conditioning.

To an individual who is wealthy, abundant resources seems like a perfectly natural experience. To the impoverished, poor living conditions are seen as the norm. To a spiritually awake person, seeing God in all things, is perfectly reasonable. To a person with vibrant health, a decrepit body is not conceivable.

All of this is due to the inner conditioning of the individualized field of being. Individualized fields of being are only aware of those objects of experience which are particular to their conditioning.

> *18. The Self is superior to the changes in the field of being. The definitions in the field of being are always known [by the Self].*

The Self is superior to all changes in the field of being. All changes and definitions in the field of being are known by the Self, which is not affected by those changes or definitions.

19. The field of being is not self-luminous because its nature can be seen.

The individualized field of being (can be considered the Soul) is the reflection of the Self, and an individualized portion of the One Reality.

The Self can only be what it is, luminous and pure. The Self cannot be perceived. We can realize we are it, and be it, but we cannot experience it. This is why mystics have such a hard time trying to explain what they know to be true. This is why it is better to follow the advice of a mystic and experience the Self directly, rather than engage in discussion about it.

Anything that can be perceived or experienced is not self-luminous, meaning it cannot exist of its own accord. It requires support. It is the Self, or the One Reality, which is the support for all perceived things.

20. Because its nature can be seen, simultaneous cognition of the field of being and an object is not possible .

Our field of being is our reference point for experience. It is like the ego, that allows us to engage in conversations with our neighbors. By pretending to be an individualized object in consciousness we can interact with other individualized objects. Returning to the dream metaphor, all the things that appear in our dreams seem separate even though they are just individualized manifestations of our psyche. This happens so that a dream can occur.

While functioning through a particular view point we can only be aware of one thing at a time. We can either be aware of the particular object, person, or place before us, or we can be aware of the point of view that allows us to have the experience in the first place. We could not function effectively, if at all, by being aware of both at the same time.

Consider that there are three aspects to the One Reality: the Seer, the Seeing, and the Seeable. The Seer is the eternal, omniscient, omnipresent, infinite. The Seer is aware of every moment, every object and every field of being. It is fully Self aware. The Seeing is the individualized field of being. The individualized field of being is aware of space and time. Space and time is the Seeable. Though seemingly different it is important to remember they are not separate from each other.

21. If individualized fields of being knew each others states this would cause confusion of memories.

Remember that nature exists to give experience for the Self. In order to have these experiences, individualization of itself into separate points of view is necessary. To have an orderly experience that makes sense, requires that there not be confusion. For this reason, we only know the states of our own individual fields of being.

22. The unchanging, pure field of awareness experiences the function of cognition upon the appearance of a form in that field.

The pure field of awareness develops its ability to "think" and "experience" when a form appears that can be thought about and experienced. When there are no forms to cognize, pure awareness remains. As yogic meditators we are endeavoring to remain fully conscious while experiencing pure awareness. This is different than the pure consciousness of deep sleep, of which we are only dimly aware. When the pure consciousness of deep sleep can be realized with full attention, we are on the right track.

> 23. *The pure field of consciousness is colored by the seer and the seeable, which is all things.*

See the third paragraph of commentary on the previous sutra 20.

> 24. *The [individualized] field of being [the seer and the seeable], although variegated by uncountable subliminal traits exists for the purpose of the Self.*

Here Patanjali reiterates the fact that the countless manifestations possible in the infinite consciousness exist solely for the purpose of the Self. The dream exists for the dreamer.

> 25. *When one sees the distinction between the sattvic field of being and the Self, the perpetuation of the false sense of self is no longer supported.*

In the early stages of spiritual aspiration devotees may be drawn to the path of Self-realization because they want to experience better circumstances, or imagine that spiritual growth will result in a glorified human condition.

Devotees may yearn to experience visions of light, and continuous moments of peace and clarity. They may yearn for the Sattvic field of being. This is a good motivation. The more we can identify with the Sattvic field of being, the easier it is to perceive reality as it is.

Sattva is much less dense then the cosmic force of Tamas, and calmer than the cosmic force of Rajas. When overcome by Tamas, it is hard to even imagine more rarefied states of consciousness. When caught up in Rajas, we are too agitated or focused on achieving something, that we miss the experience of pure conscious stillness. When Sattva predominates, the field of being is harmonized, and can now contemplate and identify with its unconditioned free state.

From this experience of Sattva we know the Self. Then we can see that even Sattva is a form of conditioning. Sattva maintains harmony, clarity and peace. Once identification with Sattva is fully released and we can maintain the Sattvic state, while existing as the Self there is no longer any confusion about our true identity.

> 26. Then the field of being is naturally inclined to discern between sattva and the Self, and is impelled onward to Kaivalya-the aloneness of seeing.

Established in this knowledge the field of being naturally flows towards complete Self-realization and then matures into the realization the One Reality, as all things, of its own accord.

27. *Even as one is naturally inclined towards to Kaiva-lya, breaks may occur due to thoughts directed to-wards objects. These are due to subliminal activa-tors that are not yet resolved.*

During the process of final realization and maturation there may be interruptions due to the few remaining sub-liminal activators being discovered and neutralized.

If we are in the final stages of realization, occasional thoughts, moods, memories, desires, and experiences may arise that seemingly draw us back to identification with our false sense of self. Remaining detached, and letting the process continue, these distractions or interruptions will resolve.

28. *These remaining subliminal activators are to be ended in the same way as the root causes of pain are to be ended.*

See Sutra 10 in the Chapter on Spiritual Practice. This sutra describes how to continue ending the remaining root causes of pain.

29. *Of the field which has continuous discernment be-tween sattva and the Self, which has no self-interest even in higher states, there is complete ab-sorption in the cloud of dharma.*

When our field of being maintains its discernment be-tween sattva and the Self, and there is no self-interest or craving for higher states of consciousness, one is then completely absorbed in the One Reality.

To have no self-interest in higher states of consciousness, means that we no longer crave what we consider to be a higher state. We can see that all of consciousness is a manifestation of the One Reality. We can metaphorically see God as all things, and so we no longer need anyone special or to do anything or go anywhere particular to experience God. God is where God has always been, right here as our very Self.

It is one thing to affirm this truth mentally, and it is quite another to experience it fully. When we experience it fully, there is no need to think about it, talk about it, or proclaim it. It is self evident, and always apparent. This is why the clearest sages say so little. To them, what everyone else is trying to experience, is obvious. This is also why the clearest sages are probably the least likely to be recognized, as they are completely unassuming.

> 30. *From that arises the ending of the root causes of pain and karma.*

When absorption in and as the Self is complete, the root causes of pain are finally and completely put to an end.

> *31. Then, infinity of knowledge dawns, which removes all veils, and little remains to be known.*

The Self is all things, manifest and unmanifest. It is involved in time and beyond time. When we have knowledge of the Self, we similarly realize knowledge of everything. This removes all the veils that block our direct experience of life as it is. After this, there is little left to know.

Then everything that is needed for our particularized life situation is available and provided. We are then Self-sufficient.

32. Because of this, the purpose of the changing cosmic forces of nature is achieved.

Then the interplay of the cosmic forces that make the experience of life possible have fulfilled their purpose.

33. Then the progression of time and its moments is apprehended at the end of its changes.

When we are engaged in reading a story, often the reasons why various literary situations happen is not evident until it is majestically tied together at the books conclusion. Then the work makes sense in its entirety. When we come to the end of our journey, identified with space-time, the progression of moments in life are understood. Life then makes sense.

34. When the cosmic forces return to their source, devoid of any remaining purpose for the Self, then there is abidance in one's own essence.

We now return to the beginning. As it was written in the second and third sutras at the beginning of Patanjali's entire work, "Yoga is the process of ending fluctuations and changes in the field of consciousness." And, "Then the Seer abides in its own true nature."

As the cosmic forces return to their source, devoid of any purpose for their manifestation, one then abides in one's own essence.

Chapter 9

CONTINUING THE LINEAGE OF ENLIGHTENMENT

Every person that has the capacity to understand and apply the principles of meditation and yoga described in the Yoga Sutras can become Self-realized. Every person that sincerely engages the process of meditation and adopts a yogic lifestyle, is continuing the lineage of enlightenment.

Even when we are unsure of how to proceed on our chosen spiritual path, we can either learn from a knowledgeable person, from a helpful book, or through trial and error. In time, our practice and application of yogic philosophy becomes skillful. Our understanding grows as we begin to directly experience what is taught within the Yoga Sutras. Sincerity, intention and commitment to our highest good and spiritual growth empowers the process.

Enlightenment is a state of consciousness whereby we know what we are at the core of our being. When enlightened we understand that we are in this world to play a certain role, yet we are fully aware of the fact that our true nature is timeless, infinite and untouched by the sorrows of the world.

Every day is the same once enlightenment dawns. In the morning we meditate deeply, giving our full attention to pure consciousness and resting in the realization of infinite, timeless being. At night before sleep, we spend time internalizing our attention, letting go of our attachment to the day, and returning once again to meditation. In the daylight hours in between, we live as best we can, fulfilling our duties, serving in our chosen role, and being appropriate to the moment.

In time, through practice, the enlightened state becomes constant. Then all moments, all places, and all people are imbued with the light of pure consciousness. We realize we are the Self of all, and all that we experience is a manifestation of our own divine being.

Yogic practices then become our natural way of being. We no longer have to force ourselves to follow the yamas and the niyamas, or make ourselves sit down to meditate. Knowing our unity with all, we are not inclined to steal or to harm another, because we know directly that we only harm ourselves. We naturally flow to a tranquil alert state, and so meditation becomes enjoyable, and the experience persists even beyond our formal sitting practice.

Then it is our joy to radiate this light to the world, and if others are drawn to us, we can share the simple practices that made our own realization possible. Or we may remain living as we always have, doing our work, and letting the light of consciousness shine through in every action we take.

In Lahiri Mahasaya's commentary on the Bhagavad Gita in Chapter 18, verse 3 it states:

"Kriya Practice, initiating into Kriya and austerities or self-restraint, are the duties of a seeker which no realized Kriyanwita (Kriya Practitioner) should renounce."

Then in that same chapter, verse 5 it says:

"The duties of a realized Yogi are to practice Kriya, initiate others into Kriya and to hold to the ultimate Self. Thereby, the mind becomes pure."

Once realized we continue our practice and assist others in learning the methods and processes.

However, to continue the lineage of enlightenment does not mean we *have* to teach techniques and practices, or talk about spiritual growth with others, it only means we maintain our inner radiance and let the Self flow through as it will. If we are called to teach, we will. Otherwise, living a simple life and continuing our private practice is enough. Through silent example the lineage of enlightenment continues.

The lineage of enlightenment is also maintained through organizations that have inspired and Self-realized leadership. Although it is important to remember that enlightenment is not found in organizations or through identifying with a particular teacher or person. It is only found through applying the teaching and living a life that results in liberation from the normal fragmented human state. Organizations can maintain the teachings and provide opportunities for learning. Teachers can share information and embody a clear state of consciousness to be emulated, but it is important to let go of the delusion that spiritual growth will occur without *our own* sincere efforts to remove the obstacles to its realization.

If we are blessed to have access to an authentic spiritual teacher, or to have the support of an organization that encourages the development of its members, that is helpful. As Lahiri Mahasaya and his students have stressed, access to an embodied, living teacher is essential, and should not be neglected. Yet we need to always remember, it is our own Self-effort, our own personal practice, that makes the process of Self-realization come to fruition. It is by our own preparation that we were able to find an authentic teaching in the first place and it is by our continued Self-effort that we are able to experience the benefits of association with Self-realized teachers.

By consistent meditation practice, making choices that are conducive to a healthy body and mind, by choosing supportive relationships, taking responsibility for providing sufficient resources for ourselves and those in our care, by providing a useful service to the world, and the study of meaningful spiritual texts our lives naturally flow towards an enlightened state. During a private visit, Mr. Davis once said, "If people would meditate daily, eat their vegetables, exercise, pay their bills on time, and love God, that would be all they need to do."

Wherever we are in life, we can take one step at a time, to make the necessary changes that clear the way for Self-realization. As the years go by, our consciousness will become clearer, because of our intentional practices, and our life more enjoyable as our spiritual understanding grows.

For every one of us that engages in the process of Self-realization, the lineage of enlightenment continues.

Appendix

Appendix A – Food List For Vata Constitution

Fruit

Apricots, bananas, cherries, dates, figs, grapes, grape-fruit, lemons, limes, mango, papaya, peaches, pears, per-simmons, pineapple, plums, pomegranate, orange, raisins, raspberries, strawberries, and tangerines are excellent.

Most fruit is good. If it is dry then soak it in water.

Raw apples, melons, and cranberries should be avoided.

Vegetables

Beets, bell peppers, carrots, cilantro, hot peppers, Jerusa-lem artichokes, mustard greens, okra, onions (well cooked), parsley, radish, sweet potatoes, winter squash, and yams are all good if well cooked.

Alfalfa sprouts, artichokes, asparagus, broccoli, Brussels sprouts, cauliflower, cucumber, egg plant, green beans, peas, potatoes, spinach, squash, tomatoes, turnips, and zucchini may cause difficulty.

Too many raw vegetables as well as lettuce and mush-rooms are to be avoided.

Grains

Basmati rice, brown rice, oats, and wheat are all excel-lent.

Barley, buckwheat, corn, millet, and rye may cause difficulty.

Dry grains, granola, and corn chips are to be avoided.

Beans

Mung beans are good.

Aduki, black grams, chick peas, lima beans, peanuts, and tofu may cause difficulty.

Fava beans, kidney beans, pinto beans, lentils, and split peas are to be avoided.

Nuts and Seeds

All nuts and seeds are good except in excess, particularly almonds and sesame seeds.

Oils

All oils are good. Almond, sesame, and ghee are excellent.

Dairy Products

All dairy products are good. Those that are sour, buttermilk and kefir are excellent.

Sweeteners

Sweeteners are all right in moderation. Natural sweeteners are excellent.

Condiments

Spices, pickles, and vinegar are excellent.

Animal products

All animal products are generally good for grounding Vata. Fish and eggs are better than red meats.

Appendix B – Food List For Pitta Constitution

Fruit

Sweet and astringent fruit is best. Apples, cranberries, dates, figs, grapes, mango, melons, pears, persimmons, pineapple, plums, pomegranate, and prunes are excellent.

Sour fruit, apricots, bananas, cherries, lemons, limes, oranges, papaya, plums, peaches, and strawberries may cause difficulty.

Vegetables

Alfalfa sprouts, asparagus, bell peppers, broccoli, cabbage, cauliflower, celery, cilantro, cucumber, green beans, lettuce, mushrooms, okra, peas, potatoes, squash, turnips, and zucchini are excellent.

Beets, carrots, chard, eggplant, mustard greens, parsley, spinach, sweet potatoes, and tomatoes may cause difficulty.

Hot peppers, garlic, onions, pickles and radishes are to be avoided.

Grains

Basmati rice, oats, corn, granola, and wheat are all excellent.

Brown rice, buckwheat, millet, rye, and corn chips may cause difficulty.

Beans

Most beans are o.k. but are Rajasic. Aduki beans, mung beans, and tofu are Sattvic.

Lentils are to be avoided.

Nuts and Seeds

Coconut, and sunflower seeds are good.

Pine nuts, pumpkin seeds and soaked almonds may cause difficulty.

All other nuts, especially roasted and salted are to be avoided.

Oils

Butter, coconut, ghee, corn, sunflower, flax seed, and olive in moderation are all good.

All other oils are to be avoided.

Dairy Products

Sweet dairy, milk, cream cheese, and cottage cheese are excellent.

Buttermilk, kefir, and yogurt may cause difficulty.

Sour cream and salty cheese must be avoided.

Sweeteners

All natural sweeteners are good except Jaggary, honey and molasses.

Condiments

Condiments are to be avoided especially spices, salt, and vinegar. Exceptions are coriander, cumin, fennel, mint, turmeric, and soy sauce in moderation.

Animal products

Animal products should generally be avoided, except egg whites and the white meat of chicken, if one wants to take them.

Appendix C – Food List For Kapha Constitution

Fruit

Dry fruit, apples, cranberries, raisins, and prunes are excellent.

Apricots, grapefruit, lemon, lime, mango, papaya and pomegranate may cause difficulty.

Sweet fruit, bananas, cherries, dates, figs, grapes, melons, oranges, pears, peaches, persimmons, pineapple, plums, raspberry, and strawberry should be avoided.

Vegetables

Astringent and pungent vegetables: alfalfa sprouts, asparagus, artichokes, beans, beets, bell peppers, broccoli, Brussels sprouts, cabbage, carrots, celery, chilies, cilantro, lettuce, mushrooms, mustard greens, parsley, peas, potatoes, radish, and turnips are all good.

Cauliflower, cucumber, eggplant, squash, spinach and tomatoes may cause difficulty.

Okra and sweet potatoes are to be avoided.

Grains

Barley, buckwheat, corn, rye, and dry grains are all excellent.

Millet, rice, and granola may cause difficulty.

Oats and wheat are to be avoided.

Beans

All beans are generally good, particularly soybean products. Tofu can aggravate in very high Kapha conditions.

Nuts and Seeds

All nuts and seeds should be generally avoided with the exceptions of pumpkin and sunflower seeds.

Oils

Corn, safflower, soy, sunflower, or a little ghee can be taken in small quantities.

Dairy Products

Goat's milk, small amounts of buttermilk are ok. Soymilk is preferable.

Dairy products should generally be avoided.

Sweeteners

All sweeteners should be avoided except cooked honey.

Condiments
All spices are good, particularly cayenne, black pepper, garlic, and ginger.

Salt, vinegar and pickles should be avoided.

Animal products

Animal products should generally be avoided. Pork, beef, and chicken are acceptable if one wants to take them.

Appendix D – Healthy Impressions for Each Constitution

Reproduced with permission from *Ayurveda and the Mind*, by David Frawley. Lotus Press, a division of Lotus Brands, Inc., PO Box 325, Twin Lakes, WI 53181, USA, www.lotuspress.com ©1997 All Rights Reserved.

The following information is meant to serve as a guideline to balancing the mind/body constitution of each Ayurvedic Dosha.

Vata-reducing Impressions

Nature: Sitting or walking quietly and peacefully by a garden, river, forest, river, lake or ocean, particularly where it is warm and bright

Sensory: Sound-calming music and chanting, classical music, and peaceful silence

Touch: Gentle warming touch or massage, using warm oils like sesame or almond

Sight: Bright and calming colors like combinations of gold, orange, blue, green, white

Taste: Rich nourishing food abounding in sweet, salty, and sour tastes, with moderate use of spices

Smell: Sweet, warm, calming and clearing fragrances like jasmine, rose, sandalwood, and eucalyptus

Activity: Gentle exercise, Hatha Yoga, Tai Chi, swimming, hot tubs, relaxation, and more sleep

Emotional: Cultivating peace, contentment, fearlessness and patience; releasing fear and anxiety, having support of good friends and family with regular social interaction

Spiritual: Prayers for peace and protection, developing discrimination and insight, meditation on the innate fearlessness of our true nature, or on strong forms of divinity

Pitta-reducing Impressions

Nature: Sitting or walking by flowers, river, lake or ocean, particularly when it is cool, walking at night or gazing at the night sky

Sensory: Sound-cooling or soft music like the sound of flutes or the sound of water

Touch: Cooling, soft, moderate touch and massage with cooling oils like coconut or sunflower

Sight: Cool colors like white, blue and green

Taste: Food that is neither too heavy or too light, abounding in sweet, bitter and astringent tastes, with few spices except cooling spices like coriander, fennel, and turmeric

Smell: Cool and sweet fragrances like rose, sandalwood, gardenia or jasmine

Activity: Moderate exercise, walking, swimming

Emotional: Cultivating friendship, kindness, and courtesy, promoting peace, forgiveness, compassion and devotion; releasing anger, resentment, conflict and hatred

Spiritual: Prayers for universal peace, cultivating surrender and receptivity, meditations on the peaceful and blissful attributes of our true nature

Kapha-reducing Impressions

Nature: Vigorous hiking or walking in a dry or desert region, high mountains, or on a sunny windy day in open areas

Sensory: Sound-stimulating music, strong, and energizing sounds, singing

Touch: Strong, deep body massage with dry powders of stimulating oils like mustard

Sight: Bright stimulating colors like yellow, orange, gold, and red

Taste: Light diet emphasizing pungent, bitter, and astringent tastes with liberal use of spices, occasional fasting

Smell: Light, warm, stimulating and penetrating fragrances like musk, cedar, myrrh, camphor, and eucalyptus

Activity: Strong aerobic exercise, jogging, sun bathing, wind bathing, saunas, reducing sleep

Emotional: Cultivating detachment, service, to others and selfless love; releasing greed, attachment, and clinging

Spiritual: Meditation on the void or inner light, prayers to experience the immaterial aspect of our true nature

Over time you may find that you naturally include nearly all aspects of the list into your daily life. When this occurs know that an inner balance has been created.

ABOUT THE AUTHOR

Ryan Kurczak graduated from Fairmont State University with a bachelor's degree in Psychology and minor in Philosophy. After college he attended the Mountain State School of Massage, and completed training with The American Institute of Vedic Studies and the European Institute of Vedic Studies in the subjects of Yoga, Ayurveda and Jyotish. He has studied astrology intensively under Richard Fish and Ernst Wilhelm.

Ryan was initiated by Roy Eugene Davis, a direct disciple of Paramahansa Yogananda. He teaches group meditation and Kriya Yoga practices, at various Yoga and New Thought Centers, and works with sincere students individually.

He lives in Asheville, NC where he works full-time as a Vedic Astrologer, offering phone and internet astrological sessions.

See: www.AshevilleVedicAstrology.com.

Other Books By The Author

The Art and Science of Vedic Astrology:
The Foundation Course (Co-Authored with Richard Fish)

The Art and Science of Vedic Astrology Vol. II:
Intermediate Techniques and Applied Chart Assessment
(Co-Authored with Richard Fish)
Available September 2013

A Course In Tranquility:
Integrating Spiritual Practice, Effective Living,
& Non Duality
Available December 2012

15592077R00109

Printed in Great Britain
by Amazon